JUST

CHECKING

JUST CHECKING

SCENES FROM THE LIFE
OF AN OBSESSIVE-COMPULSIVE

EMILY COLAS

POCKET BOOKS

New York   London   Toronto   Sydney   Tokyo   Singapore

POCKET BOOKS, a division of Simon & Schuster Inc.
1230 Avenue of the Americas, New York, NY 10020

Colas, Emily.
    Just checking : scenes from the life of an obsessive-compulsive/
Emily Colas.
        p.   cm.
    ISBN 0-671-02437-X
    1. Colas, Emily. 2. Obsessive-compulsive disorder—Patients—
Biography. 3. Obsessive-compulsive disorder—Popular works.
I. Title.
RC533.C635   1998
618.85′227′0092—dc21
    [B]   98-15001
                                                               CIP

First Pocket Books hardcover printing July 1998

10 9 8 7 6 5 4 3 2 1

For my muse, Santiago

ACKNOWLEDGMENTS

*With love to the extraordinary Eva and Adam
and gratitude to my favorite girls, Cynthia and Jane*

PART 1

STARS

I like to make stars in my head, or trace them with my finger. Just like you doodle with a pencil on the side of a piece of paper. Someone will be talking to me and I look like I'm listening, but really all I'm doing is drawing one line of the star for every one word that person says. Our conversation has to end on a multiple of 5, a complete star. My husband might say to me, "What do you want for dinner?" I'm looking him straight in the eyes so I guess he believes I'm deciding, but in fact I'm drawing and thinking 1 and ⅕ stars. He says, "How about pizza?" I still just stare at him, but think 1 and ⅘ stars. He continues, "Do you have any idea?" 2 and ⅘. Finally he'll conclude, "Why don't we just make pasta?" 4 stars.

CLEAN TIME

It had been almost a decade since I'd taken a pill and I was not thrilled to find myself about to swallow one. I just stood in front of the sink for a minute or two and then got up the nerve to stick it in the back of my throat and drink it down. I imagined the outer casing was starting to dissolve and the powder inside was filtering up to my brain. I was waiting for something dramatic to happen. Maybe I'd fall down in convulsions or start hallucinating. Maybe I'd be overcome with the urge to kill my husband.

In college, I'd had a nasty drug habit and the unfortunate experience of a bad trip. After that night, I suffered from flashbacks for a few months and vowed never to take a pill again, harmful or otherwise. When I was pregnant, I relented and took vitamins. After I had kids, Advil. Several years later, today, I was moving on to this serious medication. I was a little shaky. It was probably the drug.

IN THE BEGINNING

My husband and I went to a bar for our first date. We were pretty young at the time, both in school. We sat next to each other at a table in the back of the place. The lights were low, cigarette smoke clouded the room. Lots of atmosphere. We spent the night talking with our heads really close and our fingers twisted together. We had both just ended serious relationships so we wanted to take this slow. After the drinks, we went back to his place and stayed up for hours while he read poetry to me. Then we fell asleep, him on the couch, me in his bed.

YOU WANT FRIES WITH THAT?

I used to sit dazed at the table watching my father eat breakfast. It was always the same meal, toast, eggs, bacon and juice, which he'd always eat the same way, bite of toast, bite of eggs, bite of bacon, sip of juice. Bite of toast, bite of eggs, bite of bacon, sip of juice. My head would follow his hand around from his plate to his mouth, to his cup, to his mouth, to his plate . . . around and around until he'd finished. I'd have to shake my head and blink my eyes to snap out of my trance.

I SWEAR TO TELL THE TRUTH THE WHOLE TRUTH AND NOTHING BUT THE TRUTH . . .

You never know what kind of things people have going on in their lives. Secret things that you have no idea about. The woman who dry-cleans your clothes? Prostitute. The man who sells you coffee and a doughnut? Serial killer. And your friend who hasn't returned your calls lately? Heroin addict. And then I find out that my friend wasn't returning my calls because she was in rehab. Which I'll admit is a little jarring. I pretty much assumed that people just spill everything. I do. Maybe that's wrong. Maybe I shouldn't. How are you supposed to know what to tell and what not to tell? Maybe my dry cleaner really is a prostitute. Maybe I should stick to cotton. I feel confused. And of course bad for my friend who it turns out had been addicted to heroin for five years and was now trying to kick methadone. She says that she wanted to tell me, and almost did a couple of times, but she was just too embarrassed. I totally understand. But that still leaves this whole honesty issue unresolved.

DINNER AT SEVEN

I've often been told this story of when my family went out for a Sunday night dinner, I was seven at the time, and I started making jokes about a woman I noticed who was a dwarf. After what I assume were a few uncomfortable minutes for my relatives, my aunt, wanting to put an end to my mocking, turned to me and said, "It's not nice to make fun of people, but if you have any questions I'd be happy to answer them for you." I sat there for a minute or two with I guess a pensive look on my face and then said, "Do you think she was normal until she was seven and then she got like that?" I'm sure my aunt answered no, but that still left open the question of what I would turn into.

AND DINNER AT 7:00

For our second date, my husband invited me over for dinner. This was going to be our first problem. I'd been under the impression of late that people were putting acid in my food. The kind that makes you hallucinate. This started a few months before when I was at a party and a friend of mine was eating sugar cubes from a bowl on the table. The hostess of the party yelled to him, "Don't eat that! It's where we put our acid!" My friend got this horrified look on his face, because by that point he'd probably had about ten hits. Then the hostess started laughing. Sure she was just kidding, but something like that could happen; you might accidentally eat someone's stash or maybe some malicious dealer with an attitude wants a laugh. As a result, I had stopped going to restaurants and dinner parties and just ate prepackaged food. It hadn't affected my life too much until this point, but I liked this guy. I could see myself getting serious about him. I figured that this was going to be our first trust test. I showed up at seven.

"Hey, I'm glad to see you. How was your day?" he asked as he softly touched my arm and slid his hand down to hold mine.

"Okay." I was pretty nervous. I wasn't sure if it was second-date anxiety, fear of my impending trip or both. "How about yours?" He started talking about what he'd been up to, his classes, the paper he was working on. I was looking at him and I thought I was listening, but truly, I was distracted by the smell of the cooking food in the next room. Being reminded of what was in store for me.

"I have to go check on dinner. Can I bring you a drink?" he asked.

"No thanks. Do you need any help?" Maybe I could monitor. Make sure he didn't slip anything into the sauce.

"No, I'm good."

Twenty minutes later he brought out dinner and set it on the table. Chicken and rice. We sat down. I shuffled the food around with my fork for a minute or two and eventually got up the nerve to cut a piece of chicken and spear it when he said, "I forgot the salt." He disappeared into the kitchen and I had this dilemma. I had about five seconds to decide whether or not to switch our plates. If he had laced my food, this was going to be my last meal before I was chopped up into little pieces and hidden out back. I didn't know if I should chance it. I did want to start this relationship on the right foot, but that's pretty hard to do looking up from the ground in a thousand pieces. He seemed like a nice guy, but don't a lot of serial killers? Ted Bundy. The clown guy. But there were other considerations. If he had poisoned my food, and I switched the plates, then he would die and I'd get questioned by the police.

"Um, ma'am, we found a horse dose of cyanide in your boyfriend's food. How do you suppose it got in there?" He'd have done the bad thing, but, unable to prove my innocence, I'd end up in jail. Plus, I'm not sure the cops would be patient enough to wait for me to answer them until I had completed a star.

"Ma'am. Could you answer our questions? Why aren't you speaking to us? Do you want a lawyer? Ma'am? Hello."

8 stars. "I didn't do it. I switched the plates. I'm innocent . . ."

No. Don't think that way. Trust. Besides, he'd eaten more than I had and maybe he'd notice. I left the plates where they were. He came back to the table, sat down, and started talking to me. I listened and ate and waited the requisite forty-five minutes for the drugs to take effect. When the time passed and I wasn't hearing colors or anything, I started to relax a little.

OF COURSE OF COURSE

The first time my husband and I had sex, I thought he was a transsexual. It was about three weeks into the relationship and we were both looking forward to finally doing it. Everything was going along great until he pulled down his boxers and I glanced at his penis. It didn't look the same as the ones I'd seen before. It's not like I'd seen so many, but they're a pretty standard item. I started to get nervous and as he fumbled around with the hook on my bra, I tried to account for the difference between his dick and everyone else's. There's this old medical saying that I've heard in my travels through countless doctors' offices. It goes like this: "When you see hoofprints in the sand, think horses not zebras." Think simple, obvious. Fine, but I'm not a doctor and I wasn't with one, so I figured that this was what a penis looked like when it was sewn onto a discarded vagina. I tried to convince myself in other ways that he was indeed a man. He had no breasts or even any extra skin from previous breasts. He had a hairy chest and an appropriately deep voice. Horses. Horses. I got up the nerve to ask him about it and what came out of my mouth was remarkably composed: "Are you uncircumcised?" Bingo. That was a lucky break because I really liked this guy and I wasn't sure I was mature enough to handle the lesbian aspect of that other option. Communication is so important to a healthy relationship.

MISS CLEAN

At the end of my first summer at sleepaway camp, the counselors sent back a report to inform parents how the summer had gone for their kids. Mine read like a psychiatric evaluation: "She was very aware of time and distance. On hikes she wanted to know what time it was, how far we'd gone, how far it was back, when we'd return to camp, etc. . . . During story reading she'd ask how many pages were in the chapter. This preoccupation with time and distance continued throughout the summer." Another insightful passage observed, "She is independent about doing her cabin work. Her bed is always neat and her shelves tidy. She does her cabin work without being reminded." The next summer's report was more complimentary: "Her cubbies were kept tidy and her bed made with precision." *Precision.* What a lovely word. I should write them a thank you note.

ROUND AND ROUND AND ROUND IT GOES

My mother sent my husband an unusual birthday card. There was a picture of a fortune-teller with tarot cards laid out on a table and a crystal ball in front of her. Inside the crystal ball was an erect penis. When my husband opened the card it said, "Looks like an exciting and wonderful year for you." If that wasn't bad enough, her personal message to him was "Enjoy your BIG day!!" She claims she didn't realize what that thing was inside the crystal ball. I know she's getting old and maybe her eyesight isn't so good, but my husband had been reading a lot of Freud so it was hard not to think the worst. It was going to be tough to do something to celebrate that would top the card, so I didn't try. I just took him to dinner with some friends. We were having a nice chat as we walked along when one of our friends said, "It *is* blood. I thought so." Another friend said, "I saw it too, but I didn't want to say anything." It seems we had been following a trail of fresh blood drops down the sidewalk and into the street.

When I was in college, I took my mind off my problems by using drugs. If I wasn't looking for them or experiencing their effects, then I was recovering from them. So there wasn't a lot of time to worry about much else. But somewhere along the line I realized that drug addiction wasn't what was in store for me. It wasn't my path. And I guess as some sort of divine confirmation, I had that bad trip, and as a result, stopped using. It was like some god somewhere was telling me, "We have something else for you. Something special." I was honored. Until I realized that special treat was insanity. Don't get me wrong, I mean it in the most basic way. No hallucinations, no aliens telling me what to do. Just extreme and intrusive neurotic thoughts. And the really bad part of insanity lite is that I have most of my rational functioning intact, which makes that out-of-order part all the more unpleasant. Look, I don't want to get too hokey here, but it's like there's some sort of spirit deciding my fate. Somehow thinking about my fears over and over, hour after hour, day in and day out, appeases Him. But if I slip up by, say, not thinking enough about a worry or maybe by being bad, like hurting someone's feelings, then my spirit needs to punish me. Like by, say, leading me down a street with a trail of fresh blood drops for me to walk on and obsess about what diseases lurk there. Then the rational part kicks in and I think, "Not only am I wearing shoes that protect me, but the people I'm with are good and worthy and this happened to them too." Which makes a lot of sense. Until it occurs to me that both my soles are quite worn and I've been strolling on blood with a marxist, a lesbian anarchist, and an adulterer. So it's hard not to think the worst.

PENICILLIN QID

As we were getting to know each other, my husband learned of my randy ex-boyfriend. This all came about because of my husband's summer job. He was going to be answering phones at the national AIDS hotline. I've always had a healthy concern for sexually transmitted diseases; I even had a few minor checks at a clinic; but now, because of my husband's new position, AIDS was on my mind. I had dated that other guy for about four years and had suspected he wasn't faithful. Maybe because every time we walked by a group of girls, they'd point at us, whisper to each other, and then giggle. Maybe because he told me he'd never been faithful to a girlfriend in his life. Or maybe just because when I asked him, "Have you ever cheated on me?" he answered, "I haven't, but I wouldn't tell you if I had." After a couple of years together, he spent a semester studying in another state. I decided that our relationship needed a new beginning and this was a good time, so I called him and we agreed to tell each other about our past infidelities. Clean the slate. I went first. I had two. Then it was his turn, three. I felt so much better.

About a week after our confessions, I was hanging out with a friend of mine when we happened upon the topic of how my boyfriend and I had shared our cheating history. My pal then told me that he had already known about my boyfriend's infidelity. Here's why: After a party one night, this friend, my boyfriend, and a girl were in a hot tub together. This girl and my boyfriend were kissing and then, after a little while, they retreated to a room. That's when my friend informed me that my boyfriend had slept with this women and become a member of her club. The members being all the boys that she had slept with. It was called "The Catholic Girl Club." Actually, the club was named after the girl, her proper name, but by the time the story got to me, she had found God and stopped sleeping around. So I thought it might be a nice touch to rename the club in honor of her renewed faith. Anyway, it was all a little too late for me. Sure my boyfriend and I had already confessed, but he had neglected to mention the Catholic. I decided to call him up. I told him this story and said, "I want to try this one more time. Tell me everyone you slept with during our relationship and this time don't leave anyone out. I'm going to give you some time to think about it. Call me back in half an hour with your list. If you tell me everything, I'll let it go and we can start fresh." He hemmed and hawed, but finally agreed. Thirty-five minutes later I got a call back, a list of over twenty women, and an appointment at that clinic.

So I felt it was in my husband's best interest to inform him that I'd had sex with a man who'd had sex with the majority of girls on campus. But for the most part, I wanted to forget it ever happened. Because even though I'd been tested for many things, AIDS was not one of them. And really, I thought, wouldn't it be nicer just to not think about it for a little while longer?

THERE ARE NO ACCIDENTS

Say I'm on the phone and the conversation gets dull. Instead of thinking of an excuse to get off, I start to have some fantasy in my head. I'll still be talking to the person on the other end of the line, but after a few minutes I'll realize I've been daydreaming and I don't know what I've actually said. Maybe my kids are bugging me to hang up and instead of politely saying to them, "I'll only be a minute guys," I yell, "Leave me the FUCK alone!" When I'm done with the call, I ask my

15

- - - - - - - - - -

husband over and over, "Are you sure I didn't say anything bad? No cursing?" He's unable to convince me, so I have to wait around for a few days to make sure social services wasn't tapping my line.

This zonelike state also overtakes me when I'm writing things down. Before I'll hand someone a piece of paper on which I've written, say, directions, I'll check the page over and over to make sure I haven't put down any stray marks or hidden thoughts: "Left on Main, right on State, I'm going to kill my mother."

MY STARS!

The first fight that my husband and I ever had, a few months into our relationship, was about that summer job. I didn't want him to take it. I figured if I didn't have to hear stories about AIDS all summer then I wouldn't have to think about how I might have it. I had enough on my plate with my everyday worries. The more I thought about it the more I knew this wouldn't do. We were sitting on his porch when I innocently told him, "I forbid you to take that job!" That didn't go over too well. Words were had and I think the phrase "controlling—something or other" might have been tossed on the table. I know for sure his anger escalated to the point of beating the crap out of the mailbox. So, in the end, he took the job, we got our first AIDS test, and went on our way to couples counseling.

No Shit

When my mother was a teenager, she had a bad stomach illness and was rushed to the hospital. She had to have surgery and then spend a couple more weeks there recuperating. During that time, there were a lot of discussions about how she was doing and what the future would hold for her, now that she was missing a significant portion of her large intestine. Of course, the concern on the part of her doctors and family made sense since she was so young at the time and since it was a pretty major rerouting of her plumbing. But my mother could never quite get over the fact that these chats all took place behind her back. No one felt the need to share any of this information with her. I realize it was the fifties and things were different back then, but, come on. The whole experience really affected my mother's view on honesty and openness. For one thing, she always tells the truth. Or so she says. And just to bring the point home, my friend the heroin addict constantly tells me, "You're only as sick as your secrets." So it seems like a good practice, to tell the truth. One that I try to adopt. But it gets pretty complicated. Like, when my son looks up at me with his big brown eyes and asks, "Does Santa really know if I've been bad, Mommy?" Is it wrong to

17

say, "Yes. So you better go clean your room. And don't hit your sister." Doesn't it seem sicker to say, "I'm sorry honey, there's no such thing as Santa. He's just a mall employee."

So in the end, I try to use my best judgment. Santa gets his cookie. Rudolph, his carrot. And I plead and hope it doesn't get more difficult than this.

COUNTING SHEEP

Do you ever feel like your tongue is too big for your mouth? I was lying in bed trying to fall asleep when I started to think my tongue didn't quite fit anymore. Once I started focusing on this, it was all I could think about. I imagined my tongue was expanding in its already close quarters. My body started to tingle, I had trouble breathing, and I began to wonder if a swollen tongue would obstruct breathing through my nose as well. I tried to distract myself by thinking about small things while taking deep breaths. I toyed with the idea of calling my doctor, but felt that familiar pang of embarrassment. What would I say? Since it was so late and his office was closed, I'd have to call his service, give my name, and when the operator asked me what's wrong say, "I think my tongue is swelling." She might just laugh and hang up the phone or maybe this really happens and she'd send an ambulance over immediately. I wasn't thrilled with either option. After a few hours of going over my choices, I came to the realization that if my tongue was indeed growing, it was a pretty slow process, and I fell asleep.

THE PSYCH WARD

In college I took this course called Abnormal Psychology. We basically studied all the different mind disorders that people could get. In addition, in order to pass the class, we were required to volunteer at the local public mental institution. Which I did. The patients just sort of sat around in a fog with a vacant look on their faces waiting to be brought their daily medication. Some would be yelling out at seemingly no one and others might just spit and twitch. Then there was Patient X. She was apparently the girl who everyone feared. She was about 6 feet tall, 220 pounds, and didn't much like the college students. She would get pretty aggressive and chase them down the hall. X's reputation was common knowledge, so the students usually requested a ward other than hers. A request that was granted because it seems her reputation was deserved. Patient X liked me a lot. She followed me around, hugged me constantly, and gave me pennies. It's nice to know I'm attractive to aggressive, sociopathic psychotics.

A GOOD MAN IS HARD TO FIND

Here's what people say about my husband. They say if you made a list of all the traits you'd want in a man, my husband has them all. Really, that's what they say. And they're right. It's totally true. Let me show you.

handsome, yes
smart, yes
kind, yes
funny, yes
warm, yes
faithful, yes
good job, yes
good father, yes
good to his wife, yes
responsible, yes
trustworthy, yes
dependable, yes

After that college boyfriend, I tell you, I felt pretty lucky to have met such an amazing guy.

YOU WANT CYANIDE WITH THAT?

I let my husband in on my little secret. The one about the poisoning. He was pretty sympathetic. Since he liked going out to dinner, but didn't want to see me suffer, we made a compromise. We'd go out to eat, but he would have the first bite off my plate. The way I figured it, if he was confident enough to eat my food, then it must be okay. As if his complete and utter lack of fear would somehow rub off on me. Then again, if something did happen to go wrong, we'd trip or die together. It all seemed romantic at the time. But I wasn't sure I was going to be able to convey this feeling to him, so I was more subtle. At first when we'd go out and my plate would come, I'd make a big show of how great the food looked and then ask, "Want a bite?" He'd look up, oblivious to my scheme, and say, "Sure." I'd find a good piece, one with unidentifiable spices and stuff, and pass him my fork. It was going along great until the time we went out and I ordered a food he didn't much care for. He declined my offer to taste.

I tried again. "You sure I can't interest you in a bite?"

"No, I'm good, thanks."

I suppose I could have figured out some clever way to get the food in his mouth, but I didn't have the energy or inclination so I fessed up. I told him the acid in the sugar story, followed that up with the second-date dinner story, highlighting how brave it was of me to eat the food of a virtual stranger, and then brought the point home with, "Look, it's just a bite. It's not a big deal and it'll make me feel better. What do you say?"

At first he seemed reluctant to comply. He gave me a quizzical squinty-eyed look, slowly stammered, "Um, but, ahhhh . . ." and then exhaled really loudly. Maybe I had a pathetic look on my face, or maybe he thought he'd be curing my fear if he taste-tested, or maybe he just wanted to get on with his meal. Whatever the case, he took that bite and from then on there was no going back.

U-HAUL

My husband and I moved around a lot. I have a short attention span. First we both stayed at his apartment. It was small and not "ours," so we found a new place. To make it even. We signed a one-year lease and everything was going smoothly until I decided that it was too small. We broke our lease and found a new place. We settled in, got a cat, then two, then my husband got asthma and he coughed a lot. We needed more space. We decided to buy. We had one year left in North Carolina, but we didn't care. We broke another lease, bought a bigger place and put his study at the far end of the house. We got another cat and a dog that died. Still, we stayed put until we moved to California. In the meantime my husband got a Ph.D., I went through a few jobs, we had one kid, and gave away the cats. I hated Los Angeles, but we never changed apartments. My husband didn't get any more advanced degrees, I didn't get any jobs, but we did break our lease and have another kid. The next move was to Michigan. We fully intended to buy a house again, but needed time to look. We signed a six-month lease, found a place in two, broke the lease, and moved into our new house. I got antsy, made up some excuse like, "It's too small," and we sold the house. We rented a new place while we looked for a bigger one to buy. A few months later we separated. My husband got his own place and that led me to today, at the sink, with this damn pill in my system.

1-800-342-2437

Six months after we met, my husband and I went in for our first AIDS test. Sure we'd been using condoms, but my old boyfriend and I hadn't. So for general safety purposes, and so I didn't have to worry while he was manning the phone lines, but mostly so we could lose the rubber, my husband and I got checked out. Since this was the first test, the technician acted pretty professional. She asked us about our past sexual, medical, and drug histories, drew our blood, and told us the results would be in later that week. It was a tough few days and the beginning of the "What if . . . ?" question. "What if I have AIDS?" I'd ask my husband about twenty times a day. He was patient and tried to reassure me.

"I'm sure you don't."

"But what if I do?"

"Look, you never really did anything that risky. I wouldn't worry about it."

"You're not nervous? I find that hard to believe."

"I'm sure we're both okay."

"But what if . . . ?" It went on like that until the week was up, I called the clinic, and we went down to get our results. The technician brought us back to a private room to tell us the good news. She ended up working at the clinic for the rest of the time we were in North Carolina and we became friends. Any time I was afraid I'd been infected or got another test, like when I accidentally drank out of someone else's glass, or when some woman inadvertently spit in my eye while she was talking to me, I would call up my tech and she'd take care of me. Eventually she decided to become pregnant so she stopped drawing blood, just to be safe. But she was always willing to draw mine. I guess after all the tests I'd taken she was convinced I was clean. But I just couldn't see it. I mean, you never know.

REVEILLE

I used to throw up all the time when I was five. Every night, in the middle of the night, I would walk into my parents bedroom, gently tap my mom on the shoulder, and whisper to her that I needed to puke. She was groggy at first, but then she heard me gag and choke, so she sprang up, grabbed my arm, and tried to jerk me to the toilet. My dad, by this time roused out of his sleep, ran over to me and cupped his hands to catch what he

24

could. When I was finished, I took a sip of water and went back to bed. My dad grumbled about the mess I'd made and then fell asleep. Mom stayed up the rest of the night to clean.

QUESTION MARKS

Right out of college I worked as a substance abuse counselor at a private in-patient treatment center. It was a great job for me. Twenty-four-hour access to doctors and nurses. They answered all my questions, gave me blood tests if I wanted, and generally took care of all my medical needs. There were a couple of job responsibilities that weren't so great. Like, every time a new patient was admitted, I had to go through his suitcase and search all his clothes and personal belongings for a hidden stash or drug paraphernalia. I'd sit in this tiny room with the things strewn all over a table, put on rubber gloves, and start checking. Looking back, this wasn't the safest job in the world. Suppose I had put my hand in the pocket and, oops, a syringe. I pull out my hand and there's this needle embedded in my finger. The place could open itself up to a nasty lawsuit or I could get some incurable disease. After not too long, I decided it would be best if I quit. Now I was really stuck. Who'd answer my medical questions? I picked my husband, the literature professor. He'd be reading a book and I'd be involved in my nightly task of finding a new worry. This particular night I was taking the dishes out of the dishwasher when I noticed that the cup I had coffee in said DO NOT MICROWAVE. My husband is Spanish and in our lazy way we made his favorite café con leche by microwaving our milk. I was up the whole night certain I had lead poisoning, or worse, cancer. My husband was sleeping and I whispered his name and then: "Do you think it's all right?"

He was kind of groggy, but he said, "Huh, what? Oh yeah, sure."

"Do you really think so?" I asked.

"Yeah." He turned over, facing the wall. Subtle. I wasn't deterred.

"What if I have cancer?"

"I'm sure you don't. Go to sleep."

"But what if . . . ?"

"Go to sleep." But it was useless for that night.

The next morning, in an effort to put an end to this worry, I tracked down the makers of the cup. Turns out they were a small company in Connecticut and when I called I actually spoke to their president. I told him what I had done and he assured me that I could grind the cup down into little pieces and eat it and it wouldn't harm me. Then he offered to send me a new cup, kind of missing the point.

FAILURE TO COMPLY WILL RESULT IN PROSECUTION TO THE FULLEST EXTENT OF THE LAW

There was no secret or magic to my husband's being my safe zone. It came down to survival. Plain and simple. I needed my worry, spin, and doubt, but I also needed not to die. So I found a way for those two conditions to coexist. I'd engage in the former while my husband prevented the latter. It's not that he wanted the role so bad, it was more like an evolution. The more he helped me, the more I needed him to. And he was usually willing to do what I wanted. Answer questions or open doors or whatever. And he did it all in a logical, rational, calming sort of way without challenging this whole structure. I suppose if he had, I would have found someone who didn't. But that proved to be unnecessary. He accepted the role. So, I got what I needed and, I presume, he did as well. At least for a while anyway.

YOUR MOTHER WEARS COMBAT BOOTS

I got the name of our first couples therapist from one of the recovering-addict counselors at the drug treatment center where I used to work. I made an appointment and we went in to see him. This therapist firmly believed that a dysfunctional family is the root of

everyone's problems. The first thing he did was pull
out a huge sketch pad and put it on an easel. He looked
at me and said, "You first." He wrote my name at the
bottom of the page and then proceeded to have me
name all my relatives while he constructed my family
tree. "Now," he said, "give me three adjectives that
describe each person." Next to each name he wrote
down the words I chose. Then, to the right of my tree,
he made one with my husband. The doctor said he
would place the easel, with our trees visible, next to his
chair during all our appointments, for reference purposes. When he'd finished drawing, we had about
fifteen minutes left to talk. I was looking down, fid-
dling with a button on my shirt. I could feel him
staring at me, so I began. "We had a fight. It started
with this job my husband wanted to take at the
national AIDS hotline. I was nervous about it, so I
forbade him from taking it . . ." I was about to go on,
but was startled by this pounding noise coming from
our therapist's direction. I looked up and saw him
wildly rapping his knuckle on the pad next to my
father's name. One of dad's adjectives was *controlling.*
I guess like me. "Proceed with your story." I was
thrown. This guy was a bit too dramatic. I looked over
to my husband to get him to continue. He looked back
at me. I went on, "Well, we worked that one out. I want
to ask you about something else. I have this fear that I
have a disease. Well, actually, lots of diseases. And I
ask my husband about it and he doesn't know what to

say." I looked at the therapist, who was doing that chin-scratching thinking thing. He had an idea: "Why not, at the beginning of each day, have your husband give you a thorough physical exam. Check you out, and make sure you're okay?" My husband and I glanced at each other. I kind of giggled, wondering if he was kidding. My husband looked angry. Which led to this exchange between them. My husband started. "Her problem isn't that she has a real medical illness. We need to explore her underlying psychological disorders that merely manifest themselves as hypochondriasis."

"But the medical concerns are real to her."

"Even so, I'm not a doctor."

"But she needs to see that you care. That she can trust you."

"I'm sure there are healthier ways then a pseudo–medical exam." My husband snarled. "This only validates her symptoms." The therapist was looking over at his easel searching for an appropriate familial adjective for my husband. My husband turned to me, took my hand, and gave me a "Do you believe this guy?" kind of look. I just sat there on the couch, looking at my watch, and willing it to speed up.

THE FLEA

I wonder what would happen if you lay down on your pillow and there happened to be a flea beneath you. From the flea's point of view, this would seem to be a mighty frightening situation that he'd want desperately to escape. Of course he'd be no match for a ten-pound head. He'd have to weigh his options: die a slow and torturous death, wait patiently and hope the enormous object moved, or take action. Suppose he chose to take action. With all the strength he can muster, he wiggles around and looks for an opening. He finds one. Your ear. Thinking he's seen his light at the end of the tunnel, he makes his way through this path. Up the lobe, into the canal, past the drum and cochlea. Finally he gets to your brain. He's pretty hungry at this point so he starts eating. By the time you wake up and notice, he could have done some serious damage.

SHAKEN AND STIRRED

The heroin addict and I went to college together. Although at the time, she was just a drinker. There was this one night, though, that I was going to be doing drugs and, not wanting to have the experience alone, tried to convince her to take them with me. I was pretty persuasive and she was pretty game so we ended up tripping together.

There's this theory that claims there are certain drugs that are gateway drugs. They're the more innocuous drugs, like alcohol and marijuana. So if you experiment with those drugs, you're more tempted or more open to then go on to use the more serious, dangerous drugs, say crack or heroin. Narcotics and Alcoholics Anonymous, on the other hand, maintain there's no drug hierarchy. Addiction is addiction no matter what the substance. And no drug is worse or better than any other. I suppose my particular belief is that both views have a certain validity. Although my personal God probably favors the former theory. I figure that must be the case since my friend the (albeit heavy) drinker went on to become my friend the heroin addict. And I ended up having that bad drug trip, presumably as punishment for opening her gate.

SAY GOOD NIGHT GRACIE

I used to get frustrated at bedtime. My mother would sit on the edge of my bed, tuck me in, and kiss me good-night. Then she'd walk to the door and with her middle finger flick the light switch off. The hall light was on so I could see mom standing there a few minutes later still stroking the switch that was clearly by that time down. I'd yell "It's off!" to get her out of my room. She'd look back at me and then turn her head away, silently shut my door, and leave. Fifteen years later she explained to me that she knew the light was in fact off, but felt compelled to keep flicking the switch, in multiples of four, until it felt "right."

31

WAITER, THERE'S A . . .

My husband and I had the taste-testing thing down so I moved onto the wait staff. Who were they? Where had they been? Did they have any cuts on their hands? Did they wash them after a trip to the bathroom? I started out subtly.

"Did you see the Band-Aid on that guy's hand?" I asked my husband at dinner one night.

He looked up from his menu, by now used to the incessant interruptions during his meals. "Uh, no. I didn't," he said.

"Well, it was huge. I think he had three of them all in a row."

He smirked and said, "Do you understand the purpose of a Band-Aid?"

"He does work around sharp utensils. Maybe he cut himself setting our table." My husband looked back at his menu. I continued, "What if he did?"

"What if? What if?" my husband repeated, probably trying to figure out how to stop me. "I'm sure if he had he would have replaced the knife with a clean one."

"What makes you so sure?"

"People just don't go around leaving bloody knives on restaurant tables." He was looking me straight in the eye and could see I wasn't buying it. He picked up his knife. "Perfectly clean. No trace of body fluid. And look at the tablecloth. It's spotless. No blood stains. I'm sure it's fine."

"Ask him how he did it."

"You ask him."

"I can't. You ask him."

"Come on," he begged.

"Please."

The waiter came over to our table and pulled out his pad and pen.

"Are you ready to order?"

"Gosh, what happened?" my husband asked staring at the guy's cut.

The waiter lifted his finger and looked right at the covered wound. "Oh, I got that helping a friend of mine move. What can I get for you?" He took our order and went away.

I looked at my husband, unconvinced. "What if he was lying? Trying to cover for potentially infecting us?"

"He seems like a pretty honest guy," my husband answered.

"I wonder how long ago this happened?"

Here's my thinking. If the injury occurred a few days ago, then the cut was probably scabbed. Not as dangerous. But if it were more recent, then who knows, maybe it was leeching fluid. "Ask him . . ." I stopped talking. I realized I have a talent. I possess an endless capacity to keep a worry alive.

THAT'S THE WAY THE COOKIE CRUMBLES

My husband and I were having ice cream with our only married friends. I had a brainstorm. "Why don't *we* get married?" I asked my husband. He was understandably wary. We were only twenty-three, he was in school, and I was turning out to be a handful. I guess maybe he thought the planning would give me something else to think about, something other than my worries, so he entered into the discussion with a surprisingly open mind.

"I'd love to get married," he started. "I'm just not sure now is the right time."

"It's a perfect time," I countered. You see, I live my life according to some general theories, which I decided to reveal to my husband. I stumbled across the first one when I was snacking with a friend in high school. We were eating Oreo cookies and discussing the manner in which we ate them. I twisted my cookie open and ate the bare cookie half. Then I ate the edges of the remaining piece so that at the end, I had as much of the cream filling left as possible. Because it was my favorite part. Now my friend, she twisted her cookie open as well, but then she immediately ate the cream. Which was odd to me since everyone likes the cream best and why wouldn't you want to save it for last? To end on the most tasty note. So I questioned her about her technique and she told me what amounted to the Oreo cookie theory of life. Since the cream is the best part it should be eaten first in case the eater dies before finishing the cookie. Thereby making his last moment on earth the most enjoyable. I adopted the theory, and in keeping with it, decided it made sense to have a wedding. My husband blinked his eyes, shook his head, and relented.

COUNTING SHEEP II

I have a successful strategy to help me fall asleep. I take my pointy teeth, the canines, and find a good fleshy bit of my lip, right on the inside. Then I bite down. Hard. I hold my teeth there for a few minutes until the pain starts to subside. Then I bite down harder. In a short while, I'm asleep. I notice I do it at other times too. I'll be sitting around reading a magazine and I realize my eyes are closing. Since it's early in the day, I start to wonder why I'm so tired. Then my attention is drawn to the slight stinging sensation in my mouth. I'm biting. It's pretty effective.

FORGIVE ME FATHER

I chose October 14 as our wedding date. The ceremony was in my father's backyard. He and his wife, the one he married after my mother, planned the whole thing.

My husband and I wrote our own vows, though. Very simple and traditional, do you take this woman, blah, blah, blah, love, honor, obey, blah, blah, blah. The judge seemed fine with this at the time, but on the day of the wedding he sprang this long, sappy, spiritual reading on us. Apparently, he believed we hadn't written vows that would satisfy our guests. You can see me scowl the whole way through on the video. My aunt, who was sitting in the third row, didn't look too pleased either. She had this look of shock on her face as my father walked me down the aisle. It seems she was a little confused and thought she was at my father's wedding. So really it made sense, as my dad and I passed her by, when she blurted out, "Is that who he's marrying? I'll kill him." Although I'm not sure if it was the age difference that bothered her or just the incest.

At the end of the ceremony the guests applauded, ooohed and ahhhed, and got up to congratulate my husband and me. A business partner and close friend of my father's stayed in his seat, turned to his wife, and said, referring to me, "She's been putting a knife in her father's heart since the day she was born." Maybe it was the black suit I was wearing or that I was marrying a Catholic. Maybe he just wanted to make my aunt feel better.

* * *

After dinner, my husband and I stood in front of the guests and as my father toasted us, I cut a piece of cake to place in my husband's mouth. I guess the day was kind of distracting and I didn't pay enough attention to what I was doing. The knife slipped and cut my index finger. The very last image you see on my wedding video is me nervously sticking this finger in my husband's face for him to check it.

SWAPPING SPIT

I had my first kiss the summer I turned thirteen. It was the last summer I spent at that sleepaway camp. I had been seeing this guy for a few weeks when he proposed we take our relationship to the next step. He'd walk me back to my cabin after our nightly campfire or sing and then attempt to make his move. The first few nights all I could do was giggle nervously. Then one night I composed myself and we made contact. He opened his mouth really wide and came toward me slowly. Our lips met and it was going okay until he slipped me his tongue. It was wet and weird and most certainly did not belong in my mouth. I jumped back, stared at him wide-eyed and clearly shaken, screamed, and ran into my cabin. I thought about calling my parents for advice, but it was easier just to pretend I was sick for the next few weeks.

WHY MY HUSBAND STAYS

First, there were draws that are basically base—
things like my hair and my hands and my face.
Also my smell and my tender caress,
to him these things were important, I guess.
But the reasons go deeper I have to admit
on why my husband was unable to split.
Perhaps he's demented, a klepto, erratic,
paranoid, anxious, or plain posttraumatic.
Maybe a loser, psychotic, bulimic,
schizoid, repressed, or just hypoglycemic.
These ideas are no good, my mind is a void,
perhaps it would be wise to seek help from
     Freud.
I think that the doctor might offer this credo,
I was the id for my mate's superego.
Or from Jung's point of view, the yin and the
     yang,
maybe that's why my partner did hang.
I was his match, the piece he did lack,
anima, animus—he sounds like a quack.
So off I did roam to get resolution,
the Anonymous folks might provide a solution.
Their text would suggest that my guy's
     codependent,
his need is to caretake, to fix me, to mend it.

The shrink that my husband so often was seeing
believed something else was the cause of his
  being
this man who it seems for no personal gain,
stayed with this woman who seemed so insane.
The shrink's take was simple, yet not to bemoan,
he believed that my husband feared being alone.
And now he was with me, we were in this
  together,
there was just no other way to think of forever.
Till death do us part, our bond can't be broken,
now that those vows were so openly spoken.

BRACE YOURSELF

During a routine physical exam when I was ten, my
doctor noticed that my spine was mildly curved. As a
precaution, he had me fitted for a small brace that I
was to wear at night. I wasn't thrilled about it, but no
one knew, and it didn't alter my life too much so on the
whole, I was okay with it. Two years later, though, my
condition took a turn for the worse and my doctor
wanted me put in one of those ass-to-chin twenty-
four-hours-a-day braces. Being a gawky-skinny-frizzy-
haired thing, this was not what I believed would be my
ticket to the social big time. I thought all hope was
gone until my doc mentioned another option. There
was this experimental treatment being done in a uni-

versity research lab in the city. He thought I'd be a good candidate so he gave my mom this guy's number, she called, and they set up a meeting.

A couple of weeks later my mom and I drove into this circular driveway surrounded by ivy-covered brick buildings. The place was deceptively idyllic, for inside it was gray and stone and fluorescent. My researcher was tall and skinny with a beard, mustache, and a basement office. He was a nice enough guy and I had to hand it to him, he was trying to come up with a way to make the lives of teen girls with scoliosis more comfortable. But, when you think about it, why the fascination with budding young girls? His idea, his project, was to outfit us with a small box that would rest at our chest. Attached to that were a few wires that looped around between the legs. When and if we slouched, the box would beep until we stood up in the correct posture. There was also a button to push that shut off the beep in case of emergency. I suppose that would be a movie theater where the noise might disrupt the other patrons. I took it more loosely and just kept my finger on the button if I ever put the gadget on. Which I did only when I went in for my checkup. Anyway, it was a very delicate and precise instrument, so the right fit was crucial. It required me, at thirteen, with a lot of straight lines and bones but nothing remotely female on my body, to stand in front of this guy for two hours.

Naked. Being extremely modest, I made my mom wait in the other room while this guy and his assistant took all sorts of measurements of me. Looking back, I was probably in pretty good shape. I should have strutted around, enjoying the moment. But without the benefit of hindsight, the whole thing felt pretty icky.

I ended up having the gizmo for a year until it became clear that I was not wearing it and therefore not being a good subject for this man's research. My regular doctor noticed my condition didn't worsen during that time and so with the exception of my having really bad posture, the whole spine thing ended there.

PSYCH WARD II

After I left the drug counseling field, I moved on to psychiatry. I figured I could stay in the mental health field without having to deal with patients and therapists. Now I did research. It was just me and my computer. When I got bored, I would chat with my co-workers. One was a guy who turned out to be a bit of a worrier himself. We once got on the subject of hepatitis because a worker at a local pizza chain was found to be infected and this guy happened to have eaten there. One of the doctors who worked in the office was listening, and she told us that as long as the infected person washed his hands after using the bathroom, there was no problem. The worrier then introduced me to his theory of disease transmission: the damned if you do, damned if you don't theory. It went like this. The guy goes to the bathroom and gets the virus on his hands. As he goes to wash them, he puts his dirty hands on the spigot to turn on the water. After he washes his hands, he puts them back on the dirty spigot to turn the water off. Now the virus is back on his hands and, of course, on the pizza. Damned if you wash your hands, damned if you don't. My co-worker went to get a shot of immune globulin and I decided to quit.

EASY AS PIE

I believed that I'd found my purpose. To be a mother. Which seemed so logically to follow being married. Now all I had to do was get my husband to agree. When I posed the question to him, he was reluctant. He said that he'd love to have kids, it was more of a timing issue. A two-parter. First, he wasn't sure he was ready to handle that kind of responsibility at this point in his young life, and second, he was still in school and felt that he might not be able to devote enough time to the child. I totally disagreed. First, we'd have nine or more months to prepare. Plus, is anyone ever *really* ready? It's more like you learn as you go along. I also knew that once he got out of school, his schedule was going to get busier and there might never be a great time. Besides, finally, this was my project. My responsibility. I wanted to be the one to take care of the baby.

I don't think he truly bought my arguments, but I'll tell you something about my husband. He's a stand up, do-the-right-thing kind of guy. And sure you could pretty safely argue that this wasn't the *right* thing, but, you can't fault the guy for wanting to make his wife happy.

FOR TUNAS THAT TASTE GOOD

My theory of life was changing from the upbeat, live-in-the-moment, Oreo cookie, to a less enjoyable one. Maybe it was the enormous responsibility of gestation, or maybe just the disturbing stories I kept hearing. Take this one—a woman was eating some tuna fish, and I guess she was trying to entertain herself, so she was peeling off the label on the can. Instead of seeing silver underneath the paper, she came upon another label, the one she presumed revealed what was really in this can. The one that said Purina. Now, what are the chances you'll accidentally eat cat food? Maybe 0.001 percent. But it's a risk. So, to be safe, I became a follower of the 0.001/100 percent theory of life. If there's a 0.001-percent chance that an event can occur, then it might as well be 100 percent. And life needs to be lived accordingly. There were other events I heard about that supported this theory. Take the woman buying lettuce who got pricked by a needle hidden in the leaves. Or the man who came upon a used condom in his Big Mac.

Around every corner, behind every door, with every handshake, in every wadded-up tissue is a potential transmission waiting to happen. Do you want to rely on odds? Even good ones? And it's not like there isn't some public support for my theory. I heard recently that people who work in tollbooths have taken to wearing rubber gloves on the job. Personally I support this, but to hear it from the experts, with the exception of maybe a cold, there's nothing you can catch by exchanging money in this way. Sure the average worker might want to wear a gas mask, to protect himself from car fumes and airborne microbes, but rubber gloves? It's like I've been saying, casual contact is risky business.

MUSSOLINI ATE HIS PENIE

I was raised by a nanny. A German woman. Nanny made the trains run on time. Everything had a schedule. When you bathe: every night at six. When you eat: every four and a half hours. When you get changed:

after the meals. When you can see your parents: whenever you're bathed, fed, and changed. She lasted a remarkably long time. I suppose she also decided when you could fire her.

HERE KITTY KITTY

I tried hard not to worry, because it was really starting to wear on my husband, but new things to fret about seemed to keep popping up. Take my friend who accidentally shut her dryer door without realizing her kitten was inside. She turned it on and in an hour when it buzzed, she opened the door and found, well, Fluffy. So now I had a new thing to check. Every time I used the dryer and then the dishwasher, stove, disposal, blender, or any large appliance, I had to open and shut it countless times to make sure my cats weren't inside. This was made more difficult because I have two black cats who look remarkably similar. I'd shut the door to, say, the dishwasher and then look around the house for the cats. I'd see one, so I'd open the dishwasher to check for the other. I'd close it and then I'd see the other one. Or so I thought. I'd be about to turn it on when I'd begin to wonder if the first one had jumped in. Or if the second one was the first one. I'd open it up again and check. Still empty of felines. I was getting a headache. I came up with a solution. I found the two of them, placed them in the bathroom, and shut the door. Then I went back to the kitchen, checked the dishwasher, saw that it was empty, and started it. Then I went back to the bathroom, did a couple of head counts, and let the guys out.

ALL WE ARE SAYING

My husband's role continued to evolve. He tasted, he questioned, and now, he buffered. My pregnancy was the springboard.

"What if I get sick?" I'd ask my husband. "Then the baby might be deformed."

"I'm sure the baby's pretty well protected," he answered.

"But I can't see her. I can't know for sure."

To try to ease my mind, my husband went to the store and bought me a book. It had a lovely title. *Peace of Mind During Pregnancy*. He stood in front of me with this self-satisfied look and handed me my present. I looked down at the title. Okay, nice. But then I read the subtitle. *An A–Z Guide to the Substances That Could Affect Your Unborn Baby*. I suppose we're all entitled to our off days. The book had an easy-to-follow format. At the top of a paragraph, in bold capitals, was the generic name of a substance followed by its brand names. Then the estimated risk based on when you were exposed to that drug, and finally, adverse effects on the fetus. For example, ETRETINATE (Tegison). Known risk; skeletal and facial abnormalities, severe

46

brain defect. I felt really peaceful. This was the first book in about four years that I read cover to cover. My husband felt guilty about his error, but over time it turned out to be more like annoyance. Take a typical *Peace of Mind*–related exchange:

"Remember when I got scratched by that cat that's been hanging around the house?" I asked my husband.

"Yeah. So."

"It says here on page two hundred three that I shouldn't get a rabies shot. And if I don't get the shot, I'll die from the disease."

"Only if the cat has rabies."

"Well, what if he did?" I asked.

"Well, then you'll die."

TOLL FREE?

The phone became my anonymous link to the world. I could potentially get answers to all my questions without revealing my identity. When I worried that the main ingredients in deodorant might not be safe for my baby, I just called the 800 number on the box.

"I'm pregnant and I was looking at my deodorant and wondering if it was safe for me to use."

A feeble "Excuse me?" was all the operator could muster.

"Is it safe?" I repeated.

"You can't not use deodorant for nine months," the operator said, sounding a bit horrified.

"Actually, I'm four months along, so it'll only be five," I replied. "Can you answer my question?"

"Ma'am, women all over the world use deodorant. It's fine."

"But have you ever read the ingredients? What the hell is aluminum zirconium trichlorohydrex? That can't be good for you."

"I'm sure it's fine, ma'am."

I didn't want to push it, so I hung up. But was she really qualified to make that judgment? When I couldn't find the ingredients in my *Peace* book, I just quit using deodorant.

ARE YOU MY MOTHER?

My daughter was nine days late, but she made it. Alive and well. My husband and I brought her home, settled in, and I realized that she never cried. Since I'm somewhat moody, I thought that her silence was genetically impossible. Then I remembered something. When we were leaving the hospital with her, the nurse came in with some routine papers to sign to ensure that we were leaving with the right baby. We had to check that the numbers on my daughter's ankle band matched the numbers on my wrist band and then sign some document saying we'd done so. I was a little dazed when the nurse had us do this, so I sort of nodded and signed. I hadn't actually seen the numbers. Maybe there was a mix-up. I told my husband about my concerns and then I asked him, "What if she's not ours?"

"I'll love her no matter whose kid she is."

1 and ⅘ stars. That's helpful. I was on my own. I still had my wrist band, so I scrutinized all the pictures taken of my daughter while she was still in the hospital to see if her ankle band was visible. It wasn't. Then I tried statistics. How many girl babies were born while we were in the hospital? Did any look like her? She had hair, she was a forceps baby so she had marks under her eyes, her head wasn't cone shaped. I called the hospital to see how many hairy, marked, round-headed baby girls were born in December. You think they would have been more helpful, being used to postpartum episodes.

"Who is this?" the nurse asked.

"I just want to know if I have the right baby. Can you answer my question?"

"What's your name, ma'am?"

"How many round-headed girls with hair were born in early December?" I repeated.

"Give me your name!"

"Why do you need my name?" I was getting nervous. Like she'd transfer me to psych. I hung up. Since I didn't want to subject my daughter to a blood draw for a DNA test, I started small. I found out our blood types and they were the same. It's a pretty common one so that was only minimally useful. Then I moved to a comparison of me, as a baby, and her. We both weighed

49

the same and were the same length at each doctor visit (my mother kept a record of mine). And we both had eight teeth at six months. That doesn't happen too often. Each time I took her to the pediatrician, I'd check with him and the nurses to get their opinion. Did I look like her? Were percentiles and teeth good measures of maternity? I spent a lot of time and energy trying to uncover the truth, and slowly, finally came to believe she was mine. In hindsight, I probably should have just enjoyed the quiet.

BABY IT'S COLD OUTSIDE

The pediatrician suggested that my husband and I keep our daughter at home for the first three months of her life. No malls, no grocery stores, no contact with strangers. Prevent her from picking up any nasty germs. Sound advice. I certainly intended to follow it. He did get me thinking, though, about bugs and parasites. In ways I'd never dreamed of before. And to make it even more intense, every man, woman, and family member with an opinion on caring for a baby had a story to tell me of an obscure symptom or odd malady to watch for. Words like *roseola, impetigo,* and *varicella* came out of my mouth with ease.

I'd never paid too much attention to astrology before, because I'm a cancer. The crab. The cranky disease. Who wants to be that? But our reputation is for being mothering homebodies. So I decided just to go with that aspect of the sign and spend my days alone in the house with my kid. As much as was humanly possible anyway.

AND THE LOSER IS . . .

I was watching the Donahue show and he was soliciting tapes for a "Best Husband Video Contest." Mine would be perfect. There were four categories. Best looking. No problem. He's pretty cute. Most attentive. No contest. How many husbands taste, question, and buffer for their wives? Most unusual talent. There are so many. Checking cuts on people's hands without their noticing. Differentiating between blood and red spices in food. Getting medical histories from people with Band-Aids. And finally, most romantic. I tend to discourage that kind of thing, so who could blame him for suppressing that part of his personality. I made a video, sent it in, and he was chosen as one of five finalists to appear on the show.

FROM YOUR MOUTH

I learned all about the cold sore because of this old neighbor of ours. Chronologically old. She had one just below her lip and I was pretty certain I didn't want that in my family. So I did a little checking. Into the virus. And it's a tricky little virus at that. Maybe insidious is a better word. I read where it can live up to three hours on a surface in your home. Obviously that's extreme and conditions need to be favorable. It must be an oozing sore, and somehow that excretion has to end up on the table or wherever. But once it's there, you sure don't want to touch it. Now, our neighbor didn't have an oozer. Her cold sore was just a series of red bumps. Which is still pretty gross, but much less virulent. In the case of the non-oozing brand, contact must be pretty direct to actually transmit the virus. Say, a kiss on the lips, or some other mucous membrane. The sore is contagious for about a week, right before it appears, when there's apparently a tingling feeling, and then until it's covered by a scab. After the scab is gone, there can be a patch of fresh pink skin which looks a little spooky, but is in no way contagious. And it's pretty common. The virus. Apparently, 50 percent of people who get cold sores have their first outbreak by the time they're five.

So the woman and her series of red bumps came over. My husband offered her a glass of lemonade because it was hot out. And she accepted because, I guess, she was thirsty. I try to be a good hostess, but it just doesn't seem kosher to have herpes on my stuff. The woman was old, but still pretty sharp and I think she was able to sense my discomfort with the whole sordid affair. Maybe it was all the whispering I was doing to my husband. Then again it could have been the look of panic on my face or possibly just that I wouldn't let her anywhere near my daughter. Whatever the case, she started to get a little teary and by the time she was about to leave, it was like we had in our possession that last remaining bit of the smallpox virus. She suggested we just smash the glass and save the world from her plague. It's not like I didn't consider it, but I can impose reason. I just left the glass on the table for three hours and then ran it through the dishwasher twice.

WHO DO YOU HAVE TO SLEEP WITH . . . ?

I thought it would be lovely to have another baby around. I kept daydreaming about getting pregnant. I was sure I was going to have a girl and I was going to name her Grace. Like I was a kid playing with my Barbies and imagining what my family was going to look like. But I got pretty involved in this fantasy and as I tried to convince my husband to make it a reality, I recalled his words from the Donahue show. When asked by some guy in the audience how we keep the romance alive with the doldrums of babies and diapers, my husband replied, "Well, they're not really 'doldrums.' I mean you make this baby and you get to take care of it . . ." Like it's really romantic. I was hoping he'd get caught up in that sentiment again, but instead he sort of gave me this "Are you out of your fucking mind" look. So I wondered aloud if that whole Donahue thing wasn't a little disingenuous. But he claimed his opinion could be true without him being required to nonstop procreate. I guess that makes sense, but I still wanted that baby.

SOME DAY MY PRINCE WILL COME

When I was a kid, my father used to have me go around kissing frogs to see if they'd turn into princes. I don't recall if I actually believed this might happen, just wanted to make my dad happy, or a little bit of both. None of those options seem important enough now to outweigh the grossness of it all. But every time we saw one, without fail, my dad would say, "Do you think that one might be a prince in disguise?" and then he'd chuckle and I'd chase the little guy around, finally catch up to him, and plant one on what I believed were his lips. Then my dad and I would stare at the frog resting in my cupped hands and wait. Look, it's not like I'm building up any suspense here. Obviously nothing happened. But I kept finding frogs and I kept kissing them and frankly I'm a little concerned what this says about my ability to learn a lesson.

PART 2

RECIPE FOR A WORRY

Take one pound morbid preoccupation and mix vigorously with one cup overactive imagination. In a separate bowl, add one part hypersensitivity to three parts increased hormone activity. Fold together and let stew for hours on end.

MONTH ONE: THE DOCTOR IS OUT

My husband got his Ph.D. and then his first job, in Los Angeles. So we packed up our stuff and moved out west. During our year there we had fires, floods, earthquakes, riots, and that kid I wanted. A boy. This pregnancy had its share of problems.

My new OB's office was in the local hospital and I had trouble getting there. Every step I took I was certain that I'd stepped on blood. I had to walk around all the reddish/brown spots on the floor and try to determine their exact color. Was it more of a brown hue? Probably coffee, Coke, or scuff marks. More orange? Maybe orange soda. Or more red? Candy. You'd think the floor of a hospital would be a little cleaner. The trip would take longer because we'd have to go up the stairs. You never knew who'd get in the elevator and what would be in their vials and cups. Next I'd have to inspect the doctor's hand for cuts and hope the nurse changed the white sheet of paper after the last patient. I've also had remarkably bad luck with doctors not washing their hands and I always feel so awkward saying, "Uh, would you mind, uh, washing your hands, please?" Don't they cover that in day one of medical school? When it was finally time to be examined, they didn't really do anything anyway. They'd weigh me. I had my own scale. They'd take my blood pressure. I also had a home blood pressure kit. And they'd measure my stomach. I had a pretty good sense that it was big, so who cares. I didn't get much bang for my buck. Then I happened upon an article in a magazine. There was going to be a new 900 number: 1-900-DOCTOR. Actually, 1-900-77DOCTOR. You just call that number and for three dollars a minute you could ask the doctor any medical question. How perfect. I didn't have to leave my place or face my doctor. In addition to the blood on the floor and all the other inconveniences, there were more, better reasons not to want to go. First, because she might find something wrong with me. Second, because if she wasn't hygienic I might catch something. And third, because it was just too embarrassing to ask the doctor about my concerns. She'd just stare at me with that familiar "You know medication might help you" look. I ended up canceling most of my prenatal appointments and just chatting with my 900 doctor instead. He was a general practitioner from New York who had decided to take some time off to do this phone thing. He was really nice, but he didn't strike me as the brightest guy on the planet. He used to put me on hold all the time while he looked up the answer to my questions. Okay, maybe I wasn't the smartest caller because I let him do this. But I don't think he was trying to pad his fee, I think he genuinely didn't know the answer because after talking for a while he'd offer to call me back so my bill wouldn't be so huge. He's out of business now. I guess that's a good thing. But I have been known to dial him up in moments of weakness in the hope that he's back.

THE PEOPLE UNITED WILL NEVER BE DEFEATED

After the German, my parents hired a slew of other nannies. None were too successful. Numbers two and three had the same need for control and order as the Mussolini wannabe. With some newly acquired firing skills, my parents dismissed them in a more timely manner. The fourth one was a little careless and was let go after burning my brother with a pot of scalding water. Five was sweet, but borrowed a few thousand dollars that she neglected to return. My parents lucked out with number six. She turned out to be a winner and lasted many years. When she left us, it was her decision. She wanted to follow her dream. A year or so later she called my mother.

"I wonder if you'd be willing to write a character reference for me?"

"Of course," my mother replied. "Who do I need to send it to?"

"The sentencing board at the Bedford Correctional Facility." It seems nanny had been convicted of manslaughter and was hoping mom's letter would get her a shorter sentence.

MONTH TWO: KITTY LITTER

My brother isn't the picture of health, so I was a little concerned when he flew to LA for a visit right about the time the fetus was starting to grow all his major organs and body parts. Who knew what infections my brother would be bringing into my home. And then consequently what my son would be missing. I came up with a plan. Not horribly original, but a plan nonetheless. I had my husband occupy my brother with a tour of the local sites, the La Brea Tar Pits, Hollywood Boulevard. Finally, though, I had to face the moment when my brother and his wadded-up Kleenex came to my place. My husband parked the car in the garage that was underneath our apartment. I heard the door close, so I went to the window to watch him and my brother. That's when I noticed my brother stepping on a trail of

this beigeish-pinkish pebbly stuff. I squinted my eyes
to try to get a better look, to figure out what that
substance was. Dirty cat litter. Great. When my husband and brother got to the door, I tried to get them to
take their shoes off before coming in. My husband
obliged. My brother wouldn't. He stayed and chatted
with my husband for about an hour. I just kneeled in
the corner of the room. I was certain that the litter and
all the germs contained in it were now a permanent
part of my carpet. I was a little concerned about how I
was going to make it through seven more months. I
needed help. I called 1-900-DOCTOR. His advice was to
just "Go ahead and vacuum it up." Clearly he didn't
know about the damned if you do, damned if you don't
theory. I couldn't vacuum the carpet because if I
happened to accidentally run over the litter with the
wheel of the vacuum, then the litter would be on the
wheel, and also everywhere else I rolled it. Damned if I
vacuum, damned if I don't. I looked into having the
carpet professionally cleaned, but that was no good
because they clean carpets not with soap and water,
but with chemicals. My next move was to talk to the
owner of the cat. If the cat stayed indoors, and never ate
raw meat, then she probably didn't have toxoplasmo-
sis—the disease that could be transmitted through
dirty cat litter. It was particularly insidious because I
wouldn't show any symptoms. I could never be sure I
was infected, but while I worried, toxo would be
destroying my baby. The owner of the cat was com-

pletely apologetic about the trail of dirty litter, but less forthcoming about her cat's medical history. Sure, she admitted it was an indoor cat, but did he ever get out? This would raise the possibility of having, say, killed a bird and gotten toxo. Or did she ever leave thawing meat around the house that the cat may have licked? Another way for the cat to get infected. She just stared at me with that familiar "You know medication might help you" look and slowly closed the door on me. Since there was no way to know for sure about the safety of the litter, we instituted the shoes-off rule. Everyone who came into the house had to remove his shoes at the door, and not touch the soles since it was clear people didn't bother to look at what they step on. My husband became an expert at sliding any kind of shoes on his feet without using his hands at all.

MONTH THREE: OUCH!

I found myself at this dinner party with a bunch of my husband's new colleagues. I didn't want to go, but my husband encouraged me to make that extra effort. This was his first invite from someone in his department and he thought it would be rude if I didn't show. I was now spending most of my time worrying that people were putting hypodermic needles in my food. They would be broken up and hidden so I'd have to carefully examine each bite, thoroughly chew up my food, and then when I was certain it was safe, swallow. Not all pieces of food would pass this test, so I'd spit them out and have my husband manually inspect them. I didn't think this would go over at a party, so when people kept shoving food in my face, I had to think of ways to be polite. "No thanks." "Really, I'm fine." "I just ate at home." "I'm still experiencing a bit of nausea." But they were obsessed with feeding me and relentless in their attempts so I took my daughter to a nice quiet corner to escape. I don't think she was happy to be there either. She was just standing up, clinging to my thigh, and shoving her head in between my legs. Someone remarked that it was reconversion. "Maybe she's trying to get back in." My husband thought it was more likely that she was going in to warn her brother not to come out.

GET DOWN HERE THIS INSTANT

My parents used to love to tell me this story. We'd be sitting at the dinner table or wherever, and something would remind one of them about it. They'd giggle and Dad would begin, "Before your mom and I were married . . ." It seems Dad had taken Mom out to dinner and then back to his place for some necking. They sat on his bed, but kept at least one foot on the floor at all times. They were innocently kissing when he made his move. He took her hand and guided it down to his package. When my mother's hand stayed there, my father was shocked. This was a big thing for Mom. Pseudo-handjob. But dad wasn't satisfied and he tried to get more. As he started to unzip his pants, my mother pulled her hand off, jumped back, stared at him wide-eyed and clearly shaken and screamed, "Haven't I done enough for one night?"

MONTH FOUR: PANTY RAID

My husband brought me a special treat with the laundry; someone else's underwear. I know what you must be thinking, but it never even entered my mind. He was too busy checking, washing, and buffering to have an affair. This was clearly just a matter of negligence in ritual vigilance. He had to be punished. I needed to know when the underwear girl had done her laundry so I could determine if enough time had elapsed so all the diseases in her panties could die.

"What am I supposed to say when I knock on their door?" my husband asked.

"Just tell them you need to know when they did their wash because you lost your wedding ring and wondered if they'd seen it."

He smirked, put the wedding ring in a drawer, and set off to uncover the mystery. He found the girl, two doors down in apartment five, determined that she had done her laundry the night before, and no, she hadn't seen the ring. I thought this would be enough to set my mind at ease. It wasn't. I looked in the *Peace* book. Nothing under laundry or underwear or discharge. I called my OB to ask her if she'd be willing to test me for gonorrhea. I wasn't happy about it, but I was out of options. I needed to put my mind at rest and for that I needed to be swabbed. I don't think my doctor bought stained underwear in the laundry as a mode of transmission and she refused to give me the test. You'd think she'd have just been glad to get me in the stirrups.

MONTH FIVE: IF IT'S NOT ONE THING IT'S YOUR MOTHER

My mother became obsessed with the idea that my husband and I should go out on a date. When she was in town, she kept pestering me with her offers to babysit so me and my guy could have some quality time together. I agreed, to get her off my back, but now was not the time to worry about my relationship with my husband. I had a fetus to protect. But I left my screaming daughter with Mom anyway, my husband brought the car up to the front of our place, and we just sat there for an hour.

"Do you want some food?" he asked me.

Yeah right. Do you know how hard it is to find something suitable to put in your mouth? First you have to wash your hands hygienically, make sure they don't get contaminated, don't touch any foreign objects. Then you have to stand in front of the eatery until someone walks in or out so you don't have to touch the door. There's no contact with other people, which I guess is easy enough until you get to the retail clerk. Which sets a whole new series of rituals in motion. First, locate the healthiest looking one, inspect her hands for cuts, her mouth for cold sores, and give her the general once-over to evaluate her infectiousness. Second, the food. It has to be well sealed and absent of those pesky hypodermics. If you can manage to get out of the store safely, then the food has to get back to me untainted. "No thanks." He tried to chat a bit, but frankly I was only interested in what sort of contamination was occurring in my house while I wasn't there to monitor. It seems I lucked out while I was on my date. My daughter never stopped crying, so she and my mother never left the sofa. And I came to the conclusion that it would be better if I just stayed inside for the rest of the pregnancy.

MONTH SIX: THE TOOTHBRUSH

My husband and I got into a fight. Words were had, things were thrown, and at the end of it all the one casualty was my toothbrush. It was lying there under the broken glass and dirt from the light bulb that had been smashed by the shoe my husband had thrown. He was about to go away to a conference and since I would be stuck at home without my link to the outside world, he had to spend the day stocking the house with all the items I'd need. Then he had to check that all the food and boxes were safely sealed. When he'd finished, I quizzed him to see if he'd followed proper procedure.

"Did all the boxes check out?" I asked.

"Yes."

"Did you go over them all?"

"I said they checked out. That means I did."

"Did you wash your hands?"

"I'm not an idiot."

"What if . . ."

He snapped. He was pacing around the house, cursing and spitting. There wasn't much he could say so he just picked up that shoe and hurled it. We both watched it fly across the room and hit the light. Then we watched as the small bits of glass showered down on my toothbrush. I looked at my husband. He looked back at me. We both knew what had to happen. He went over to the sink, washed his hands, slid on his shoes, and left to go get me another toothbrush.

Thirty minutes later he, unbelievably, came back. He had six new brushes that he felt on preliminary examination looked suitably sealed. Now it was my turn. I held the package up to the light at many different angles so that I could see if there was a tear in the outer plastic. After that I'd check to make sure the folds were tacked down. I had my husband watch every step to ensure that I hadn't neglected to perform a test. I'd gently probe the plastic fold to make sure it was really stuck, and then I'd look up at him, lift up my eyebrows and he'd look back at me somberly and nod. Then I'd proceed. I'd gently open just the top and slide the box with the toothbrush out. I'd place the sealed box on the vanity while I did my next test of the plastic. This was the hardest test to pass. I'd gently run the water, fill up the plastic wrap, and make sure there were no hidden leaks. Usually there were, at the bottom corner, so I'd start from scratch until one finally passed the leak test. Then I just had to do the routine check of the inner carton, which was usually sealed pretty well. I'd make him open his mouth so that I could brush his teeth in case the bristles had any germs, a throwback to that romantic trip-or-die together notion, and then I had my new brush.

CONDOMS AND DENTAL DAMS

When my parents split up, my father was transformed into a horny seventeen-year-old boy. He'd go on lots of dates, bring the woman home, and in the morning, over coffee, tell me all the new positions he'd tried. Eventually he remarried and informed me of his good fortune.

"I got to sleep around with lots of women before all these sexually transmitted diseases came about."

I was tempted to tell him that, in fact, they've been around for centuries, and a trip to the health department could be in order, but really, I just didn't want to talk about my dad's dick anymore.

WHAT IS GROSS?

Picking boogers from your nose
wiping them onto your clothes
hocking spit onto the ground
stepping on a slimy mound
hair where it shouldn't be
toilet seats covered in pee
dirty diapers, smelly gases, leaky holes, and
    wiping asses
doing chores, clogged pores, oozing sores, sex
    with whores
roaches, ants, and pesticides
toxic waste and cyanide
cum that's dripping down your chin
getting stuck with a bloody pin
a witch's hex, a wart, a boil
anal sex, an unclean mohel
abscess, pimple, pustule, fester
dressing up in polyester
mental illness, medication
psychiatrists and sanitation

a lick, a suck, a fist, a bite
a discharge stain
insanity lite

MONTH SEVEN: DO YOU TAKE THIS WOMAN?

My husband and I generally kept a pile of about twenty garbage bags in one corner of our apartment. Which may seem out of character, for me to let them stay, but it was our trash and I knew nothing bad was in there. It was the communal trash that made me shake. So when it was time to take the bags out to the dumpster, my husband had to follow a whole hygienic procedure. To keep the neighbors' germs out of our place. First the water had to be turned on and left that way because if he touched the garbage and then the spigot, the spigot would get contaminated. Next he'd take one bag in his right hand and open the door with his left. Then he'd shut the door behind him and lock it so that no one could get into the house. I guess I could have monitored, but he wanted me upstairs so I couldn't critique him. He'd take the bag down, stand a few feet from the dumpster to be sure not to touch it, and throw the bag in. Then he'd unlock the door, open it, slip his shoes off, come inside, and wash his hands. He used a pump soap so that he could use his clean wrist to pump some in the palm of his hand and not contaminate the dispenser. The water would stay on, and he'd move on to the next bag. He went through this procedure twenty times, once for each bag, until they were gone. If contamination occurred at any point during the process, say some brown liquid was on the outside of one of the bags and it got on his shirt, and I saw it, I would not be happy. I'd have to go over the scene again and again in my mind until I could find the way to convince myself that I wasn't really in danger of getting a disease. I'd inspect myself for cuts that the brown liquid might have gone into, go over the list of things we'd thrown out in the past weeks that could have been brown, or try to remember if anyone had come into our house who might have thrown something away, like a bloody tissue, that could have gotten on me. If I couldn't shake the fear, I'd ask my husband to go through the discarded trash to find the contaminated bag and try to identify the liquid. He was usually pretty against this, so I had to beg. It was all I'd talk about for hours, and I guess in an effort to just shut me up he'd relent. Of course, this trip was considered highly unsanitary and called for special protective measures. He had to put on clothes that he'd be willing to get rid of and carry paper towels so his hands wouldn't touch the bag directly. When he was finished with his inspection, he had to take off his clothes outside our front door, leave them to be thrown away, come in, and do a double hand wash. Then I'd turn the shower on and he'd finish cleaning off. I'd sit on the edge of the bed and wait for him to finish so he could deliver his report. On this day, he identified the liquid as hamburger juice. A particularly insidious liquid that is close to the color and texture of human blood. My husband said he smelled it and tasted it and was sure that it was indeed from a cow. Looking back, I'm a little surprised that it was four more years before we separated.

MONTH EIGHT: HALF A DOZEN OF ANOTHER

Our apartment was kind of a mess. The floors were covered with a layer of dirty cat litter. Thanks to the trail. The counters, sink, and tub were covered with grime and dirt because we couldn't use toxic cleaning materials, and then there was the pile of dirty clothes, because of the laundry incident. I had this struggle going on in my head. I wanted to shower, but I wasn't sure I should. If I did, my towel might hit the floor and get cat litter on it. Then I'd get that disease and my son would die. If I made it safely through that part of the process, would I even be able to find a clean pair of panties? How many times would I have to wash my hands? Open the bathroom door, wash my hands. Open the dresser drawer, wash my hands. Wash them wrong, wash my hands. Could they handle this? Or would they crack and bleed from the stress? What if I went one more day without a shower? Would that be okay or would some germ or bacteria from my filthy body sneak into my womb and contaminate the baby? Fucking damned if you do . . .

MONTH NINE: MADAM I'M ADAM

Now that it was getting close to his birth, I had to seriously consider what to name my son. The task is pretty daunting. I mean you're saddling this kid with some tag that's going to follow him around for life. I wasn't sure I was up for the challenge so I asked my husband for help. Who, depending on how you look at it, was either extremely accommodating or excruciatingly useless because he just said, "Whatever you want." And generally I appreciate that sort of deferring to my judgment, but this wasn't the time. I needed a name and I needed his help, so I took out our baby name book and started reeling some off. He got the hint and participated. And our job was harder this second time around because not only does our son's name have to go with our last name, but also with his sister's name as well. And there are other considerations. You can't pick the name of a person you used to know, but didn't like. Because of the negative association. You can't choose the name of a past partner or fling, and you certainly can't select the name of a blood test or medical condition, like Elisa, the HIV test. Or, like the woman my friend told me about who named her newborn twins Syphyllis and Gonorrah. I guess you could always just give your kid a nickname like Baby or Honey and then when he's old enough let him choose his own name. But at what age do you trust a kid with that kind of responsibility. It has to be before school starts so his friends and teachers have something to call him. But I can picture how that'd go: "These are my kids, Pocahontas and Simba." I really felt stuck. Until I came up with a way to narrow down my options. I'd name my kid after a dead relative, in memory. Thankfully I didn't have too many dead ones, so it came down to my grandfather or my grandmother. F or A. And I couldn't think of one name I liked that started with F, so Grandpa was out and I concentrated on A names. There were a couple that I liked, but was able to eliminate for various reasons. For example, Aaron, which I think is quite nice, but didn't sound good coming out of the mouths of my New York relatives. And then it hit me. I could name him after the first man. Sort of like a symbolic gesture that we were going to have a fresh start.

MONTH TEN: PLAY DATE

My son seemed to be heeding my daughter's warning and staying put. Nine months and one day, nine months and two days, he was starting to get on my nerves. My daughter wasn't too sympathetic. In fact, she was quite demanding of my time.

"Mama. Play! Mama. Ball!"

Give it a rest. I took to turning on the TV and placing her in front of it. She was pretty responsive. Any time a commercial with a baby came on, she'd say "Baby baby" over and over while she touched the little face on the screen. Like she actually believed they were her friends. Since she didn't have many real ones, because we rarely left the house, this sort of kept my guilt at bay. We'd talk all about her playmates and which ones we might see that day. She always got excited about the Huggies boy. She thought the Pampers girl was a real hoot, but she wasn't interested in seeing little Mr. Fisher Price. He never shared his toys.

THE THIGH BONE'S CONNECTED TO THE . . .

My OB didn't make it to my son's birth. I suppose in fairness to her I should mention that I got to the hospital and was practically ready to go. But in defense of me, I should also note she lived only a couple of blocks away. I think if she wanted to be there she probably could have made it. I'm sure I wasn't her favorite patient, but I should at least get points for being most memorable. In her absence, I was forced to reexplain all the hygienic procedures the doctors and nurses needed to follow. To start, I didn't think it was wise to put the box of rubber gloves right on top of the container where you dispose of dirty needles. It seemed like a conflict of interest. I had each new nurse on duty bring me my own sealed box of gloves and place it where I could keep my eye on it. Then I had to make sure that everyone washed his hands thoroughly, and used only sterilized instruments. When I had my daughter, they were pretty laid back about everything. "Try not to use drugs." "Breathe." "Enjoy the experience." I really wasn't, so I asked for an epidural. They thought I'd regret it so they offered me narcotics. I accepted because there's nothing like mind-blowing pain to make you conveniently forget antidrug vows and whatnot. My daughter was born ten minutes later, and frankly, quite stoned. She slept in my arms for four hours straight. Now, in LA, I was getting the big sell. I had probably about half an hour to go, but they were pushing drugs on me. The anesthesiologist came in and said, "You know, I've delivered plenty of babies while I'm giving the injection. Just say the word and we'll do it. It's never too late." I'm not against anesthesia in general, in fact, I think body numbing is a pretty smart thing to do considering the circumstance. But I was a bit nervous about the risks. If my daughter slept so long after a little bit of dope, maybe my son, after an epidural, would be paralyzed. I had to beg off. My son ended up being rather large, but definitely awake and mobile. I kept my eye on him, checked the numbers on our ID tags a few times, and got the hell out of there. The whole hospital experience lasted less than twenty-four hours.

* * *

The next day, my OB called me at home. She said she wanted to congratulate me, but I think she just wanted to be sure I wasn't going to come to her for my six-week checkup.

FAR OUT MAN

A few months after our son was born, my husband got a job in Michigan. We needed to get out of our lease, which under normal circumstances wouldn't have been a problem. We had a nice place in a nice part of town. But I didn't want some stranger coming in to look at it, touching my things or using my bathroom. I had a panic attack just thinking about it.

"What if this guy has some disease and he brings it into our house?" I nervously asked my husband.

"I thought we were going to be done with the worries now."

I guess I had led my husband to believe that the only reason I was placing these unreasonable requests on him was that I was concerned about harming the fetus. And once our son was born, I would be off the hook, and so my husband could be too. But even though I wasn't pregnant anymore, I didn't feel better. I couldn't make the thoughts go away. At this moment, though, I couldn't be bothered with all that. All I could focus on was an odd man coming to our place and I needed my husband's help. "Well, yeah, but this is different, he's a stranger."

"I can't do this anymore."

"But what if he has a disease? What if he's bleeding?"

My husband got this horrible, scary look on his face. He started to walk toward the door as he yelled, "Then you'll fucking die!" and slammed it behind him.

The landlord didn't know about my concerns, not that he'd care anyway, but my excuses—the kids are sleeping, my husband has the flu, blah, blah, blah—prevented him from bringing people in to show the place. When he wised up and showed up with a potential renter unannounced one day, I had to act quickly. I chained the door and pretended I was asleep and didn't hear him ringing the bell and pounding on the door. After several days of this, the renter decided against our place. He said I had bad karma. This really disturbed me. I pride myself on my karma. I called everyone I knew and they were all happy to assure me that my karma was just fine.

LIAR LIAR PANTS ON FIRE

When I was in high school, I was pretty obedient. I was never late, I didn't drink, and I kept my room clean. There was this one time, after my parents separated, that my friends and I stayed at my dad's new place. After he went to sleep, we decided that we wanted to go see a porn movie. We could have just left since there was no way my dad was going to wake up, but to prove to ourselves we were really delinquents, we stuffed pillows under the sheets to make it look like we were in bed. As if we were so practiced at deceit that we knew all the ins and outs of fooling our parents. We got to see our movie, and the added bonus of a few men masturbating, and then went home. Part of me felt like a rebel, but most of me felt guilty. Like I said, I'm just not comfortable in the role of the scammer. But I guess as I get older and life gets more complicated, I'm learning that sometimes honesty isn't the best policy. Sometimes the truth shan't make you free. Sometimes you need to weave that tangled web. So in order to create a harmonious home environment, I decided to become a liar. I stopped telling my husband about my worries.

PART 3

HOME SWEET HOME

We settled into midwestern life and bought ourselves a cozy little Dutch Colonial. My husband purchased a lawn mower and a hibachi. The kids enrolled in the local school and our neighbors baked us cookies. Then there was me. My first task, now that I was turning over a new leaf, was to pick a career. Since I like formality and rituals, I decided to become a lawyer. You always call the judge Your Honor. When you make objections you say, "Objection, Your Honor, relevance" or "Foundation" or "Leading." That's the way you're supposed to do it and that's what everyone does. I looked into the local law school, studied for the admission test, and started to fill out the application. I was just about done when I came across the question "Have you ever been convicted of a crime?" Frankly I didn't know. I'd had two run-ins with the law, both in college. The first one was at the airport on my way home for my father's wedding. I was walking through the metal detector when one of the security guards decided to go through my bag. Unfortunately there was an empty cocaine vial in the side pocket. The guard found it and called over a policeman, who took me to the corner to have a little chat. "You and I both know what this is, young lady. We could send it to the lab to be analyzed, but it's quicker if you just admit it, sign this piece of paper, and go on your way." I did, I did, and I did.

The other time was a year later when my friend borrowed my car that had expired license plates. She got stopped and ticketed. I told her not to worry about it, that I would pay, but she insisted. I didn't think about it again until the officer came to my door to arrest me. It seems my friend had forgotten about it and when you don't pay, you're expected to show up in court on the appointed date, presumably to dispute the fine. So the judge called my name, I didn't answer, and he issued a warrant for my arrest. The officer came to my place, took me downtown, and had me talk to the magistrate, who told me to pay the fine and then go home. I did and I did.

I wasn't sure if either of those episodes counted as convictions. I called the local police department and the guy who answered the phone said that I should call the state where these transgressions occurred to find out. He also said that it's not too bright to sign a piece of paper without knowing what it says. I think, by this point, I'd already learned that lesson. So I called the DA's office in the state of my mishaps, gave the woman my name, and she printed out my record. It seems the ticket was there, but in North Carolina that didn't count as a conviction. Since she too didn't know what I had signed at the airport, she couldn't help me on that score. So I called the airport and they put an end to my worry. Apparently stuff like this happens a lot. All I signed was a piece of paper that said the airport was taking possession of my belonging, the empty vial, and I agreed to it. It seems I was in the clear and I put "no" in the crime conviction box.

Over the next six months as I was waiting to hear back from the school, my desire to go started to wane. Law school seemed a little too intense. In April I got this phone call: "Hello. This is the dean of admissions at the law school." He kept talking about how my GPA from college had been low, but my letters were good, and since I lived in town he wanted to meet me, to judge for himself. I was still on the fence, but I figured this visit might help me decide so I went to his office. He started the meeting by telling me that he was leaning toward letting me in, and I guess somewhere in my mind I was thinking, "Well then, I'll show you why you shouldn't." I lost my personality as well as my ability to string five words together, but that could have been explained away by nerves. What's harder to explain is why when asked, "How come you should get into our school instead of another person with your same numbers?" I replied, "I uh don't know. I mean, uh I uh really didn't pay much attention in uh college so I uh probably don't uh know as much as uh most of the other uh applicants." What a loser. I suffered through forty minutes of this before he finally let me leave. As he walked me to the door, all he could do was mumble something about the unusually cold weather we were having. All I could do was wonder why I'd given up drugs. This new leaf thing was going to be harder than I thought.

IF YOU KNOW YOUR PARTY'S EXTENSION PRESS 1 . . .

My mother would often repeat to me the theory on child rearing that she learned from the pediatrician I went to as a kid. It went like this: "Any idiot can raise a baby." Sort of like a bare bones, all-it-takes-is-food-and-shelter-and-they-grow kind of thing. I guess the fact that she repeated this to me so often meant it gave her a lot of comfort. Or maybe it was a slam on my parenting. Nice mother. I mean, given the circumstances, I think I'm a really good mother. I'm usually extremely patient. My friends even compliment me on that. There was only that one time when I happened to lose it and I yelled at my kids when I hadn't quite hung up the phone correctly. And I briefly believed my ranting had been recorded on the other end by Social Services. But it turns out that I was wrong and my slipup in fact was not recorded at all. Anyway, my husband assured me that even if it was, cursing at your kids is not grounds for their removal from the home. Maybe having your phone call almost taped by Social Services isn't the brightest thing, but it certainly doesn't make me an idiot. And even if I am an idiot, I'd like to think I'm not just any idiot, but a rather special one.

OH MR. SUN SUN MR. GOLDEN SUN PLEASE SHINE DOWN ON ME

In the past few years there have been an unusually large number of solar eclipses. This really throws a wrench in my day. I have to sit in bed, under the covers, with all the shades drawn, until the episode is over. Which I could handle since I like to be in bed. But I have kids. I needed to parent. With the first eclipse, my daughter was still taking naps. I got her really tired, had her skip her morning nap, and then made sure that she slept through the whole experience. I sat by her crib staring at her to make sure her eyes remained closed. Which they did. When the next eclipse came I had two kids and they were both in preschool. I felt I should keep them home because I wasn't sure I could trust their teachers to keep my kids' gazes on the floor. We would have sailed through the whole experience with the shades drawn, but we have skylights, so I needed a backup. Plan B—I tried to interest the kids in playing in the closet. They wouldn't have it. Plan

87

C—I called my husband to learn which direction the sun would be facing so we could go to the other end of the house. Since I didn't want him to know we were hiding out, I told him that I was putting a pinhole through a piece of cardboard and I needed to know where to stand to get the best view. He told me where to go and then I took the kids to the opposite end of the house. I kept them there as long as possible, but not ones to make my life easy, they kept asking for things.

"We're hungry," they whined.

"Can you wait half an hour?"

"No!" I left the safety of the north end of the house, commanded them not to move, and went to the kitchen, where the skylights loomed above me. I consciously kept my head down and got them a cookie. I returned and was greeted with more whining.

"We're thirsty." Don't they have foresight? I went back to the kitchen and got some milk. This time, though, the darkness of the day overwhelmed me and I glanced up at the sky. As soon as I did, I knew I'd made a huge error. The only thing left to wonder about now was when I was going to go blind. To put my mind at ease or to fully enjoy the time I had left with sight, I called my eye doctor to get the facts about eclipse blindness. But the nurse wouldn't let me speak to him anonymously, so I hung up. I had to come up with another option. While I was listening to the news to see when the eclipse was going to be over, I realized they had an expert on who might know the answer to my question. So I called up the station and they let me speak to some guy who was taking care of the expert guy. And he said that although it's not too common for people to look up, apparently they got a lot of data back in the sixties when some kids took LSD, stared at the eclipse, and several hours later started to go blind. So I just had to make it through the rest of the afternoon and then I'd be okay.

THE LIVING HELL OF NEATNESS

When I can't handle the world, I clean it. Which wouldn't be a problem, except I've come to visit my mother and I think I can safely say that in all the years I've known her, I've never seen so much as a piece of lint on her floor. I'm at her place trying to figure out how I feel about basing a significant portion of my marriage on a lie. Trying to figure out how I feel about not telling my husband I'm still worried. But I need a clear head and for that I need to clean. So I wet a paper towel anyway and started to wipe the floor, but it came up spotless. Then I took out her Dustbuster to go over the floor, and the buzzing noise did sort of soothe me, but without the pleasure of watching filth get sucked up, it just wasn't enough. I needed an idea. I sat down on the floor, and started twirling my hair around my finger while trying to come up with one. After a few minutes of this, I noticed that there was a nice pile of my shedding hair around me. Perfect. So as I tidied up that mess, I came to the conclusion that our lives had become calmer without the constant interruption of my worries. And our house is cleaner too. You know, to tell you the truth, lying isn't as hard as I thought it would be.

YOUR FORTY-FIVE MINUTES ARE UP

My husband goes to analysis four days a week. Lying down on a couch, free-associating:

> *Doctor:*   *Hat . . .*
> *Husband:*   *check.*
> *Doctor:*   *Coat . . .*
> *Husband:*   *check.*

Pay . . . check.   Cross . . . check.   Hip . . . check. Rain . . . check. Bounce . . . check. The works. I think it's helping my husband see things more clearly.

LIQUID HANDCUFFS

Before I decided to give up on law school, there were a couple of weeks when I was anxiously waiting to hear if I'd gotten accepted. Since this was my first real attempt at being a productive member of society, I had a lot at stake in their wanting me. To break up my day, I divided it into three parts: the morning—nervously waiting for the mail to arrive; mail time—sorting through the mail to see if my letter had come; and evening—sulking because I hadn't heard. To give myself something else to think about, I started cutting my hair. I have really thick, wavy hair that I wear straight, so it's a challenge to get all the layers even. A full haircut would usually take me about an hour depending on how thorough I wanted to be. I'd wet my hair and then put a ton of hair junk on it so it would be slick and straight. Then I'd take out my hair-straightening gadget, which works like an iron, to flatten my hair even more. Next I'd section off different pieces, put them up in clips, sit myself in front of the mirror, and try to cut a straight line. Since this wasn't so easy to do, I could spend the next several days trying to even out the scraggly pieces. By the time I had cut off five inches and given myself layers and short bangs, I decided it was time to hide the scissors. I made my husband do it so I couldn't sneak a snip. I had my moments of weakness when I pathetically begged for a fix. He never gave in, and I started getting better. I even decided to try a real hair cutter. I figured that was better than cutting it myself. Like those methadone maintenance programs. It's not as good as not doing it at all, but it's safer than doing it on your own. Not to mention, there's a professional involved.

EDDIE PUSS

I used to be obsessed with my brother. A sort of backwards Oedipus thing. Or maybe that would be sideways. Anyway, I used to follow him around, do whatever he asked, and dream of our wedding. I don't think my love was reciprocated. Or maybe it was just tough love. He'd yell at me to stop following him and his friends around. Or slam his door so that the "no girls allowed" sign was showing. I couldn't read yet, but I got the picture. When he did pay me some attention, it was just to torment me by repeating everything I said back to me, or make me drink a glass of pee. I decided it might be wise to switch my attention to someone a little more receptive. I moved on to Archie, the comic book character. I'd buy all the issues and when they were offered, send away for the large special issues. They were a little pricey, but worth it. The only real down side was that it took the standard six to eight weeks for delivery. I'd mark the calendar and tick off the days until I'd have my boy-friend. One time the six to eight weeks came and went and no Archie. After a few more weeks, I was a wreck. I couldn't eat or sleep and I sunk into a depression. My father sprung into action. He sent a threatening note on his lawyer letterhead informing their company that if I didn't receive my comic he'd take legal action.

Archie arrived within days. I suppose that could have been evidence that my father was the one worthy of my complex, but it just never occurred to me.

GOD GRANT ME THE SERENITY

Now that I was scamming my husband into believing I was better, I had to go out on a date with him. The first thing I had to do was find a sitter. I picked our neighbor who had baked us cookies when we first moved in. She was happy to oblige. But there was still a problem. I didn't want her in my house touching my things or using my bathroom. What if she cut herself and got blood all over? What if she has a sexually transmitted disease and got it on my toilet seat? Who was going to answer my "What if . . . ?" questions? I came up with a plan. Right before she came over, I put markers all around the house so that I could monitor her comings and goings. I took all the knives and sharp instruments and put them in one drawer. Then I closed the drawer and sealed it with a piece of masking tape. That way if she got into the drawer I'd know since the seal would be broken. Next I went into the bathroom. I tore the corners off the end piece of toilet paper. If she went to the bathroom, I'd know since the tears in the sheet would be different. But what if she didn't wipe? Then I wouldn't know. I had an idea. I put a small piece of blue string in the bowl and that way, when she flushed, it would be gone and I'd know of her presence in that room. If she didn't flush, then the string would be green. I also wrapped up our toothbrushes in a Kleenex, taped them, and drew a line in black over the seal and onto the paper. Then I hid them in my sock drawer. If she found them, opened them, and used any of them, I'd know. I threw away my razor and had my husband take out the trash, so the bag would be empty and I could easily see if she threw anything bloody away. I could still convince my husband to take out the trash, because no matter what my mental state, in my mind, this job belongs to the husband. Plus, I let him do it one bag at a time because we didn't have a communal garbage site, like we did in LA. Then I went upstairs to get ready.

When we got to the restaurant, we were joined by this other couple. It became stunningly clear rather quickly that I was extremely out of practice socially.

"So, what do you do?" the male part of the couple asked me.

"Um, uh, nothing?" I stammered.

My husband put his hand on mine, smiled at me, and said, "That's not quite true, love. You take care of the kids."

The female part chimed in, "Oh, that's a tough, demanding job. And certainly the most important one there is."

I have trouble buying that. Sure, the hand that rocks the cradle and all, but it seems like the only people who make that claim are the ones who are really doing something with their day. It's hard to feel like you're productive when you smell like Play-Doh and you can name all the kids who hang out with Barney. My husband and the couple kept talking and the conversation got pretty lively. I don't think anyone realized that I didn't say much the rest of the night. I wanted to, but every time I formed a sentence in my head, it just came out in unintelligible mumbles, like I was having a stroke. I'd make a grunt and all eyes would be on me. I'd get a knot in my stomach and I could feel that my face was getting hot under all that pressure. I'd try to start my sentence, and then I'd "um" a couple of times, and my husband would jump in and talk for me. He was pretty good at it, so I quit trying to chat, and just listened to him. When it was finally over, it wasn't really over. I had to go home, quiz my sitter, and check my markers.

"How'd it go?"

"Great," she said. "They were really sweet. We played and read stories and—"

"Did you need to change any diapers?"

"Nope. No accidents. We had a great time. I put them to bed around eight. But I couldn't find their toothbrushes, so they didn't brush. I hope that's okay."

"No problem. Thanks a lot." I gestured for my husband to give her the money and she left. He went upstairs and I did my next go-round. I started in the kitchen. The drawer was still sealed shut, so I pulled off the tape. I went over to the trash to throw it away, but not before I checked to see if the can was still empty. It was. I turned off the lights and went upstairs. Our toothbrushes were still lying untouched in the drawer. In the bathroom, my tears were still in the toilet paper, and my string was still in the bowl. And still blue. I flushed it with my foot, turned off the light, and went to bed to perform my conjugal duties.

ONE POTATO TWO POTATO

My period was back in my life. I'd been pregnant for so much of the past few years that I never got it on a regular basis. I'd forgotten what a bother it was. To make matters worse, I remembered a conversation I once had with a friend's mother who was a gynecologist. She told this story of how a woman came to see her complaining of a worse than usual odor. Apparently, without realizing it, this patient had left a tampon inside her for a couple of months. I recalled this because I had bought a box of maxi pads which was supposed to contain ten, but had only six pads inside. Thus began the period counting game. Opening the box had always been a ritual all its own. No tears or dents, sealed flaps, blah, blah, blah. But now there was an added step. The counting. First, after the package was safely opened, I counted the number of pads inside to see if there were as many as Stayfree claimed on the front of the box. If there were, then great. If not, then I'd have to dispose of the box, in case there had been some sort of tampering that I hadn't noticed, and instead put toilet paper in my underwear. Now, Tampax, they proved to be more of a problem. First there was the counting. But then there was the gynecological problem. I had to save all the wrappers and then the used tampons to be sure I hadn't neglected to remove one. So at the end of the already hellish period week, I had to go through my bag of trash. Counting game II. All tampons, used and unused, applicators, and wrappers were lined up on the floor and then totaled to ensure that they were all present and accounted for.

IF RAPE IS INEVITABLE

I went to meet my husband for a cup of coffee. I got there early so I could check things out without him noticing. I found a table, glanced to make sure it was clean, pulled the chair out by kicking it with my shoe, looked at the seat, and then sat down. I'd brought a piece of the newspaper to entertain myself while I waited, so I opened it up and had a look. I glanced up and saw my husband coming toward me, so I put the paper down and smiled. When he got to me, he kissed me on the cheek and then pulled his chair right up next to mine. He was in between classes, so we only had about ten minutes. We just joked around a little and then it was time for him to go. He took me by the hand and led me out. I realized I'd left the paper on the table and I suppose I could have left it there, but that might have looked suspicious, made me look like a coward, so I turned back and picked it up. I glanced at the part that had made contact with the table to see if there were any marks. And I noticed, as it seems is always the case, that there were. Three brown streaks. I kind of laughed like, figures, which caught my husband's attention and he turned and asked what was going on. I showed him the spots. To which he replied, "Yeah, so you got coffee on the paper, so what?" He knew I thought it was blood and he also knew that I wasn't supposed to care about these things anymore. And he sure as hell knew that even if I did believe it was blood and even if I did care, I sure as sure as hell wasn't supposed to ask him about it. So basically he preempted the whole thing with that coffee comment. Which tells you a whole lot about my husband.

PRESCHOOL WARD

I was invited to spend the morning at my daughter's preschool as a Mother's Day celebration. All the kids sat in their chairs, involved in repetitive games, tasks, or songs—molding balls and balls of clay; drawing or painting one circle after another after another; building blocks, knocking them over, and then building them again; singing the same short song over and over so that each child's name could be included. "My name is Mr. Yellow Bird, Yellow Bird, Yellow Bird. My name is Mr. Yellow Bird and who are you? Tony, Lindsay, John, . . ." Some were yelling out at seemingly no one. Others might just spit and twitch. And then all that cleaning up and scrubbing down. Which, of course, I normally don't have a problem with. It's just that for some reason the whole experience left me a little unsettled.

ROSES ARE RED

It was definitely a mistake to go to the Macy's Thanksgiving Day Parade. We were in New York visiting my family and so I had extra people pressuring me to go. I was confused. I knew it would be nothing but trouble for me, lots of folks, lots of commotion, lots of germs. But I did think it would be fun for my kids, so in what I look back on as a moment of weakness, I decided to go. I did sleep in because I thought adding fatigue to the mix would make me more stressed, so we were late. As we were walking up Central Park West, we noticed that the crowds were walking in the opposite direction. Indicating that the parade was no longer in the place we were now going. I didn't care. All I wanted to do was get inside so I could be clear of all the people, trash, and flying toilet paper. I couldn't take a step without encountering something red on the ground. When I was a kid in New York, all we had to eat on the street were pretzels and hot dogs. Food that was readily identifiable. Now, vendors sell the fanciest things with cherries, berries, jelly, and other crap that's way too close to the color of blood. We finally made it to where we had to go, but not before I had inspected the bottom of my shoes. There was a mushy red object there. Maybe a cherry, possibly a finger. The kids watched the parade on TV and I had a nice new worry. My kids don't even remember that lovely November day, but, lucky for me, I do.

THE APPLE DOESN'T FALL FAR FROM THE TREE

I'm not fond of Barbie. The little bitch sheds her sparkles and hair all over my place. Like I don't have enough cleaning to do. I figured the only sensible thing would be to get the kids out of the house and dispose of some of their crap. I got out a trash bag and started to throw away all toys and dolls that were small or had shedding parts. My husband came upstairs to try to stop me. By that point my bag was filled with McDonald's Happy Meal treats and glittery outfits. He grabbed the bag out of my hand and started to put some of the things back in the toy chest.

"You can't throw that stuff away," he snapped. "You know their favorite thing to do is load all these toys in a bag and carry them around."

I was tempted to ignore him and then it hit me. My kids' games were sort of like junior cleaning. So what if they didn't actually take their bag full of trash out to the curb to be picked up. It was a first step. I decided my husband was right and I put the toys away. Far be it from me to interfere with their healthy development.

CEREAL KILLER

One morning I decided to eat a bowl of Cap'n Crunch's Crunch Berries. If the stock boy is careful and doesn't mishandle the merchandise, cereal is usually a pretty well-sealed item. There's the outer box, solid, cardboard, sealed well top and bottom. Then inside, the plastic package that contains the cereal. I used to only eat a cereal called Fruit & Fibre because in addition to all the other safety devices, the inner bag wasn't glued to the bottom of the box. So I could pull it out and inspect it for various forms of tampering before opening it. But you can only eat a cereal called Fruit & Fibre for so long before returning to a more satisfying variety. And in that moment of weakness, when I needed a well-sealed sugar rush, I found myself with the Cap'n. His inner bag was glued to the bottom of the box, but I threw caution to the wind, poured myself a bowl and ate it. It wasn't until later that I realized that the toy prize inside wasn't where it was supposed to be. Instead of being inside the plastic bag, it was actually between the box and the plastic. I'd never heard of this and it had never happened to me before so I panicked. I called the Cap'n's 800 number printed on the side of the box. The woman who answered did admit that the prize should have been in the bag, but tried to cover for Quaker by saying it was probably some error by one of the machines. I wasn't buying it. I figured someone had broken into the box, poisoned the cereal, put the toy outside the inner bag, but still inside the box, maybe as some kind of calling card, and then glued the flaps shut. Even though on occasion I could still convince my husband to help me through a worry, I was mainly trying to delude him, so I came up with someone else to help me. I had this friend who I liked a lot and I thought if she could eat the cereal, and feed it to her family as well, then it must be safe. I called her and asked if she would, knowing full well that it may have been tampered with. She agreed and they ate it. We all survived and I gave her daughter the toy prize to show my gratitude.

HERE'S TO GOOD FRIENDS. TONIGHT IS KIND OF SPECIAL

A high school friend came to town with her husband and kid for a visit. While her son napped, the guys went out for beers and my friend and I sat down for a catch-up chat. She had recently started working again, now

that her son was a little older. Part-time. As a therapist.
I figured that since she was an old friend, since I was
still worrying, and since she was now a professional,
she might be a good person to confide in. But before I
began my story, I asked her to please keep the information to herself. Not to tell anyone, because frankly, I
was a little embarrassed by what I had become. She
agreed and I started spilling my guts to the girl who
used to color her hair with mustache bleach and dance
around her house singing "Tainted Love." She turned
out to be quite sympathetic and it was nice having
someone to talk to honestly, which since we moved to
Michigan, since I was lying to my husband, I hadn't
been able to do.

That evening, we arranged to meet for dinner at a
restaurant, and the seven of us, me, my husband and
kids and her, her husband and son, sat down for a nice
little dinner. Her son, however, wanted no part of the
meal and started squirming and whining. So my friend
decided to take him for a little walk. The rest of us
ordered and were having a nice enough time when we
heard this crash, followed by a few seconds of silence,
and then a lot of screaming and crying. I looked up and
saw my friend running toward us with her very un-
happy and very bloody toddler. My friend was visibly
shaken by the whole incident, and partly blamed
herself for turning her attention from her son at just

the moment he lost his balance. Someone suggested we bring our food back to my place, so the kids would be more comfortable and my friend could calm down a bit.

Twenty minutes later we were all enjoying dinner at my home. Her son had recovered from what turned out to be only a minor cut on his lip, and was wearing a new, bloodless T-shirt that his mother had brought along. But my friend just couldn't shake her guilt. Or at least that's my rationalization for what happened next. She told me she wanted to talk and took me into the other room so we could be alone. She started off nice enough by asking if the blood all over her son had disturbed me. I was touched by her concern for my well-being, and truth be told, it had, so I admitted as much and added I was glad she had thoughtfully changed his stained shirt. Wrong answer. Apparently, she assumed I was insulting the life-giving liquid coursing through her son's veins and implying it harbored yucky things. And, sure, I was, but in a purely pathological, not personal kind of way. That didn't matter to my friend. She started yelling at me and hyperventilating and then after about fifteen minutes of this, gathered up her clan and stormed out. I was stunned. I just stood there wondering how dinner and a cut turned into bash the hostess. I tried to make sense of it, but all I kept going back to was that honesty thing. I just can't quite seem to figure that one out.

PARTY TIME

My son had three of his favorite friends over to celebrate his third birthday. Everyone was excited, having a great time, enjoying the day. My son, on the other hand, spent the entire party on the sofa with his bottle and blanket. After the party was over and our house was clear of the guests, he jumped around the living room and recalled the party in the excited stutter of a three-year-old. "An an I I I played wiff wiff Andwew an an an Maffew an an I I colored . . ." At this age, kids' memories of events can be completely different from what actually, truly happened. So I figure if I just tell my kids cool stories about things they never did, eventually they'll believe they had a great childhood. Next Thanksgiving we're going to Disneyland.

IF I SAID YOU HAD A BEAUTIFUL BODY WOULD YOU HOLD IT AGAINST ME?

My husband and I were lying around in bed one night. I was watching some show on TV and he was reading a book. He used to work in his study at night, after the kids went to bed, but I thought it would be better if we spent some time together. Just the two of us. He totally agreed, apologized for being so overwhelmed by his job responsibilities that he was neglecting me, and brought his book to bed. To be with me while I watched TV. So we're lying around in bed, him in his boxers, me in a T-shirt and underwear, the kids asleep in the next room. Him and his book, me and my show. Then he puts the book down on his chest and looks over at me. I feel it, but I don't look back. He keeps it up for a few minutes, so do I, and then he puts his hand on my chest. It doesn't feel bad, so I let him leave it there while I watch the TV. After a few more minutes he turns his whole body toward me. I stay on my back, but I turn my head and look at his face. I keep staring at him, trying to figure out what he's thinking. He pulls off our underwear, gets on top of me, and then inside me. He's kind of groaning and I wonder if he's completely forgotten about what he was reading, or if he keeps the subject in his head to distract himself, make it take longer. I feel his body getting hotter, my T-shirt wetter, his breath deeper. The whole thing takes about ten minutes and I'm pretty glad when it's over. Then he goes back to his book, I bite my lip, and fall asleep.

WHY? WHY? FOR GOD'S SAKE, WHY?

It's not like I don't want to stop. Well maybe there's a small part of me that doesn't, but for the most part, the biggest, hugest part, I do want to. It's just that whatever I try, be it sheer will or mind games or therapy or reassurance from my husband, whether I pray, make pacts with God or try to be a good mother, the thoughts will not go away. And lately, there's this added component. I have this general feeling of uneasiness. Like there's something important I need to do, my life may be on the line, and I cannot remember what it is. So I stay anxious and distracted all day and then when I get to go to sleep, to possibly escape, I have nightmares. It sucks big time.

IT'S A BIRD, IT'S A PLANE

My new hobby is vacuuming ants. We have a roof infestation of carpenter ants. Apparently they've been in our house for at least three years. I know this because some of them have wings so they can swarm and mate. A highly evolved process. Not to mention the sheer volume of them. I'll be talking on the phone or doing the dishes, and I see one walking across the floor. My eyes become fixed on him and I get in this trancelike state. I go to take out the vacuum cleaner. It's a green Royal that stands upright. It looks old-fashioned in a way. I lift it out of the pantry, unwind the cord, and plug it in. I pause to enjoy the last seconds of silence. Then I flick the switch and watch as the ant tries to race away from the intense vibration he must suddenly feel on the floor. It's hopeless though and in a second or two he's gone. Then I vacuum up a few dead ones that I notice lying around, just for good measure.

HIT AND RUN

I hit a chipmunk. I was driving home from dropping my kids off at school when I noticed this small thing run out in the road. I tried to swerve and I thought I had missed him until I felt a little thud and looked back in my rearview mirror. He was shaking and by the time I turned the car around to get to him, he was dead.

When I was little, my mother hit and killed a dog. She found the owner, told him what she had done, and tried to make amends. She was completely devastated by the event. I think she took it harder then he did. If you ask her about it today, she still gets teary. The first thing I thought of as I left the scene of the crime was that dog. I thought that maybe I should have a severe emotional reaction too. I mean, I had just killed someone's child. But that didn't bother me. What I did wonder though, was if it was indeed a chipmunk. I drove back and he was still lying there. I studied his face and body, yup, he was an animal. But when I got home, the animal picture in my head got fuzzy and I had to keep going back to make sure it wasn't really a person. I watched the news to see if there had been any hit-and-run accidents in that area of town, and finally tricked my husband into coming with me to verify that

108

he was indeed a chipmunk. I know it's a really small animal, and I should have been more confident he was a rodent, but it happened right near my kids' pre-school, so you never know.

IN SICKNESS AND IN SICKNESS

The TV was on and I wasn't paying attention as I went to turn up the sound, so I was shocked to notice what was on the screen while my hand was still on the volume button. A guy who had obviously been in a fight was kneeling down, spitting blood into the snow. I froze in fear for a second and then became obsessed with the idea that I had somehow contracted a disease from this television encounter. So much so that I was unable to keep it to myself. My husband had always been able to rationalize my fears as either an unusual personality quirk or some hormonal pregnancy prob-lem. Not to mention that he believed I was better. But at this moment, he was no longer able to differentiate me from any other crazy person. That night he paced around the house in disbelief; biting his nails and shaking his head from side to side saying, "You don't really believe that, do you? The show was taped months ago. There's no way that any disease could live that long in the air. Besides there's a screen between you and the blood." 7 stars.

IS THAT A POWER RANGER IN YOUR POCKET OR ARE YOU JUST GLAD TO SEE ME?

My son started noticing his erections and informed me of this by screaming, "My penis is fat! My penis is fat!" Apparently this was not a good thing. In an effort to comfort him, I told him that if he stopped touching it then it wouldn't get fat. Look, I don't have anything against masturbation, but since its fatness was disturbing him, and I didn't see it getting thin while he pulled on it, I thought the gentle suggestion to lay off was sound. My husband didn't think this was a particularly good piece of advice. "They get fat for lots of reasons," he told me in a not-too-nice tone of voice.

The next time my son went into his "it's fat" routine, my husband wanted to handle it. He calmly said to him, "That's called an erection. I get them, you get them, all men get them. They're perfectly natural." Clearly my three-year-old didn't care about this aspect of physiology. All he wanted was for me to lie next to him in bed and for his "penis to be soft." I wasn't exactly flattered by the implication.

THIRD TIME'S THE CHARM

My brother wrote a story that got published in *Screw* magazine. Several months after that, *Screw* offered him a job as an associate editor and he happily accepted. My father appreciates my brother in a way, but I think Dad has this fantasy that he has a regular son, one who works eight to six in a nice suit, like his friends' sons. My brother didn't care, this life was just fine for him. Unfortunately for me, I became the son my father never had. He was so pleased when I decided to go to law school. Every time he talked to me he would ask in the excited stutter of a sixty-five-year-old, "Did did did you hear from Michigan?" I was going to tell him that I didn't get in, just to save myself some trouble, but instead I fessed up and told him I withdrew my application. It wasn't pretty. He kept calling me and saying, "Were you nice to the dean? Here's what you do. Write him a letter and tell him you changed your mind." Then when he started to get the idea that I was serious about not going, he switched to "Are you sure you won't reconsider?" I think somewhere in his mind he's debating having another kid.

MY DAD'S BIGGER THAN YOUR DAD

My friend and I were trying to figure out which of our lives sucked more. She started:

"I'm a heroin addict, I have to go uptown every morning to get methadone, I've been arrested, I'm thirty pounds overweight, and I can't get my drug addict boyfriend out of the house."

I countered, "You can detox, the charges were dropped, you can lose the weight, and just tell him to get the hell out. I, on the other hand, am stuck in my house. If I do go out, I have to examine every spot, leaf, and twig, I can't touch people, I worry obsessively all day and I'm sure I have a disease and I'm going to die."

"But you can get medication and then you'll be fine," she said. "I'll always be a drug addict."

"Even medicated, I'll always have these fears."

At that point my husband stepped in and called it a draw.

CHEW AND SWALLOW

My father used to be afraid to fly. Since he had to do it often, he started taking Valium to calm his nerves. When he'd arrive at the airport, he'd go over to the water fountain and take his pill. He'd time this so that the pill would start working right as he was about to board the plane. After going through his routine one time, there was an announcement that his plane was going to be leaving late. He panicked. He went over to my mother, grabbed her by her jacket lapel, and with fear in his eyes cried, "What am I going to do? I already took my Valium." I guess it hadn't kicked in yet.

This story pretty much sums up my main concern with taking medication to make myself better. First I'd need to be numbed by the drug to work up the courage to take the drug. I mean, I've heard the stories about some of the more damaging side effects. Some people actually got crazier on the drug and killed their spouses or bosses. In court they blamed Prozac, but the jury has yet to buy that argument. Even I can recognize that being a murderer is worse than being crazy. Being a medicated crazy person would be okay as long as the medicine works, but being a crazy medicated killer would really suck.

★@!#★@!#★@!#★@!#

After the bloody TV incident, I was in big trouble. My husband wanted to talk. He had really bought my scam and believed I'd been worrying less. Maybe he just wanted to believe it. It hardly matters because now he was clear. I wasn't better.

"Why didn't you tell me?" he asked.

"I don't know. I guess it just seemed smarter to pretend nothing was wrong."

"You don't really believe that do you?"

"I guess I sort of did."

"So what are we going to do now?"

"There's not much we can do," I answered.

"What about therapy?" he asked.

"I hate that."

He upped the ante. "What about medication?"

"What if I kill you?" I countered.

"Then you'll go to jail."

"What if I have a bad reaction to it?"

"Then you'll die."

"Seriously?" I said.

"Seriously, you have to do something."

"Okay," I said.

"Okay, what?"

"Okay, therapy," I concluded.

THE APPOINTMENT

I covered my hand with my sleeve, opened the door to the waiting room, and stood around until it was time for my session to start. The therapist came out to introduce himself. I stayed back so I wouldn't have to shake his hand. Then he led me to his office. He had this big gray suede chair for me to sit on, which was

good, because it was easy to inspect for stains. None. I
sat down.

"So, what brings you to my office?" he asked, I
suppose, empathetically.

I sat there silently for a minute or two trying to figure
out the best way to answer him, I suppose, honestly.
But, where to begin. I closed my eyes, opened my
mouth, and tried to just force something out. "It's sort
of like, well, I'm really afraid. Like can't leave the
house afraid."

"You mean like agoraphobia? Fear of open spaces, of
being in public?" He asked.

"No, not that. More like fear of touching people, of
getting a disease from them. I know in my head this
doesn't make sense, but I can't stop worrying about it.
I'll walk by some random person on the street and out
of nowhere this thought will pop in my head, like,
maybe he had a bloody nose. Then I'll spend the rest of
the day checking my clothes and skin for blood and
cuts. Some proof that I had or hadn't been exposed.
And I can't think about anything else. So it's gotten to
the point where I can't be around people. I can't
chance being exposed to something. I have a husband
and kids. It's getting in the way. I don't know what to
do. And I don't really want to be here, but my husband,
he wants me to come."

I looked up at him and studied his face. He was
processing. I gave him some time.

I'D WALK A MILE FOR A CAMEL

The exterminator came to get rid of our ants. We decided on a local company that would spray one time only instead of the well-known chain that wanted to come once a month for a year. Our guys seemed nice, but not too technical.

One would say, "Do you see any?"

To which his partner replied, "Yeah."

Then the first, "Are they the big ones?"

And again, "Yeah."

I wasn't too impressed. They advised me not to clean for a while after they sprayed, or else I'd wash up the chemicals. I'm not sure they realized whom they were dealing with. After they sprayed, I noticed a whitish coating along the baseboards. A constant reminder that there was a toxin in my house. I wouldn't walk around barefoot and anything that dropped on the floor by the walls was contaminated. I was low on cigarettes one day when I accidentally dropped one in the film. I thought about throwing it out, but, I was low, so I ended up smoking it. So I sat there, smoking a cigarette, worrying about the cancer I was going to get from orally ingesting a pesticide.

SEE YA

The therapist was ready. He began, "Have you ever heard of systematic desensitization?" He looked at me for some kind of response. I let him go on. "Slowly, when you're comfortable, I'll get you to start doing some of the things that you're afraid of. Like touching doorknobs or sitting in a chair without checking it. Then, when you're comfortable doing those things, we can move on to say, touching a person, and when you're ready, deal with the blood."

"How are you going to fix the blood thing?" I asked.

"I'm not sure. Maybe we can get you to touch blood that's 'safe.' Like in a test tube. And then somehow real blood."

Oh yeah. That sounds like an excellent idea. Maybe I can assist in a surgery, but without gloves. Then I'll be cured. I actually engaged him in conversation like he wasn't the one who needed therapy for coming up with an idea like that.

"I'm not afraid of 'safe blood.' I touch my kids' blood all the time. It's blood with diseases that I'm afraid of, and I'm certain you'll never get me to touch that."

"Well, I think I'll have a better sense of your fears if I actually spend some time with you outside of the office and observe you. When are you free?" He took out his book to see when he had some time.

"Why don't I just give you a call," I said as I walked out the door and never looked back.

I PLEAD THE FIFTH

My husband was curious how my session went. As soon as I came in the door, he started hurling questions at me. I wasn't ready. I needed to be alone. To think. I shut myself in the bathroom and started to clean. As I wiped up the hair and dust on the floor, I went over in my head what had happened during my session. I had to reassure myself that I hadn't been exposed to anything while I was on my get-well trip. That the therapist didn't have any cuts or cold sores. That he couldn't have known ahead of time why I was there. That he hadn't already begun his desensitization and planted some blood in the room. Then I needed to figure out a way to convince my husband that I didn't really need therapy. But he wouldn't stop pounding on the door and it was way too distracting for me to do any productive thinking.

THANK YOU SIR MAY I HAVE ANOTHER

Scars are great. They're this outward symbol of some personal pain. Just by looking at someone's scar, you know that person has suffered. Usually, or maybe almost exclusively, medically. But what about the suffering insane? We have no scars. That's why we have to make them ourselves. My friend the heroin addict introduced me to this. She'd been off drugs for a few weeks, but still needed that little something extra to get her through the day. She found that cutting herself did the trick.

"It's so calming," she would say to me.

I decided to give it a shot. I took out a knife, sat down on the kitchen floor, and picked out a nice spot on my forearm. I was skeptical, but she usually knows what she's talking about, so I continued. I did it gently at first. My skin's pretty dry, so I made a nice white line up my arm. But when I licked my finger and wiped it along the mark, it disappeared. I tried again, a little harder this time. It was extremely painful and I didn't feel the least bit pacified. I decided I'd stick with my already existing scars. The one on the inside of my mouth from the biting and my episiotomy.

DEAREST MOMMY

My mother told me that one day when she was in kindergarten, the girl sitting next to her in class had drawn a beautiful picture of a cow. Everyone gathered around the girl to admire her drawing and the teacher was going on and on about it. My mother was clearly not thrilled her neighbor was getting all this attention. So Mom leaned over the girl's desk, and with black crayon drew lines up and down the page while saying, "Let's put your cow in jail." This is not my personal recollection of my mother's artistic ability. We used to sit with a coloring book open, one page for each of us. As I crappily scribbled in Snow White's dress or whatever, my mother would be darkly outlining Dopey with one color and then lightly coloring him in with another. It looked pretty good from where I sat. I couldn't quite put my finger on exactly what I was feeling, but it was something like "I want to slug you bitch." I purposely draw out of the lines when I color with my kids. I think it makes me a better parent. And really, at the end of the day, isn't that all that matters?

TILL DEATH US DO PART

When a conversation begins with the phrase "We need to talk," you basically know you're not in for a great time. I've had two like that which really stand out in my mind. The first one happened when I was thirteen. I wanted to spend the night at a friend's house and for what I felt was no good reason, my mother said no. When I pressed her, all she would say was, "Your father and I need to talk to you." I guess I didn't take her too seriously or I was more concerned with my social plans, so I didn't let up. That is until she repeated, in a scary tone I'd never heard her utter before, "No! We need to talk." Now I was nervous. I generally don't consider myself to have a particularly vivid imagination, but I had no idea what they'd need to say that was so darn urgent. So really all I could do was imagine. And I recalled my mother telling me that when she was first married, she had a really hard time getting pregnant. When she finally did, she miscarried. After several more unsuccessful attempts, she had my brother and then a couple of years later she got pregnant with me. A short time into it, though, she started to bleed and the doctor prescribed this drug to save me called diethylstilbestrol, DES. Which may not sound familiar because it was subsequently banned. Apparently it tended to cause cervical cancer in the daughters of the women who took it. But it also had what I consider a more horrifying side effect. I had heard that some of the babies born to these women were hermaphrodites. Which is not the kind of thing a skinny, awkward, prepubescent wants to hear. "Honey, your father and I thought it was time you knew that when you were born you were both a boy and a girl and since we already had a son, we thought it would be nice to have a little girl so that's what we made you." When I got home, I found my parents sitting around the dinner table looking pretty somber. They asked me to sit down and called my brother to the table. The four of us just sat there silently for a couple of minutes until my father finally spoke.

"Your mother and I are separating." At once I got

both this enormous smile on my face and this equally large knot in my stomach. Sure I wasn't a hermaphrodite, but this didn't seem so great either.

The second remarkable "We need to talk" chat was eerily similar to the first, but with a yucky twist. Over the course of several days, it was clear that my husband was trying to sort out this lying/worrying thing going on around him. Since I wasn't going back to that therapist, he didn't see much of a way out for us. We did toss around the idea of couples counseling again, but after a few stressful days he called me into his study and said those four unpleasant words. Which were followed by three more I could have lived without: "There's someone else." It seems my husband was interested in one of his former students. He told me this now because morally, he felt he was incapable of starting something with her while he was still involved with me. And what my husband clearly wanted to do was to see her. So he left.

. . . SO HELP ME GOD

A few of my good friends had proof that my college boyfriend was being unfaithful. One lived down the hall from him and saw a constant parade of women coming and going from his place. Another, my boyfriend's roommate, later confirmed that the parade of women was indeed spending the night in my boy-

friend's room. One at a time I presume. None of my
pals however felt the need to share this information
with me at the time. I recognize what a tricky spot they
were in, but it might have been nice to know. Then
again, what good would it have done me? I'm not sure I
was in any position to end that relationship. He was a
really good-looking guy, and at the time, that was an
extremely potent part of my attraction to him. Forget
the fact that I pretty much figured he was a cheater. Or
that we didn't really have anything in common. Or that
he had a tendency to yell at me really loudly. Basically,
looks were as deep as I went back then. And it was
important enough that I wasn't ready to trade him in.
So my friends were having this discussion behind my
back. And maybe that was the worst part. That people
knew something I didn't. And were regularly talking
about it. I know there's a pretty passionate debate over
whether or not to tell one partner that the other is
cheating. And with all the back and forth, there's
really no good answer. There's the kill-the-messenger
fear. And also, I suppose, the fear that you're making a
choice to alter the course of someone else's life. But on
the side of telling, there are real disease concerns, and
of course the desire to let a friend make the choice to
remain in a relationship having all the facts at her
disposal. It ends up being a pretty personal choice. And
truth be told, I was cheating too. But it was retaliation
cheating. Which I guess is a pretty lame excuse. Besides, my closest friend, the one the other friends in

the know thought should be the one to tell me, told me how she agonized over her decision not to tell. And to this day she feels bad that she didn't let me in on it. Now that I have a somewhat more spiritual outlook on life, I tell her that it must be that she wasn't supposed to tell me because of the lesson her not telling me was meant to teach me. So I was trying really hard to figure out just what that lesson must have been. All I can think is that when your partner is interested in another person, it sucks a lot more if you care about him beyond his appearance. So I tried to look deeper, because that one's basically a lob. And there is that talking behind my back part. Which really bothered me. So, I figure that whole situation helped to make me a more honest person. Which I guess was nice to be reminded of since I'd gotten so good at this lying thing.

IF AT FIRST YOU DON'T SUCCEED

Over the years I've received some helpful bits of advice to get me to abandon my unproductive ways of thinking. My husband always tried to appeal to the rational part of me. "You know this isn't how the world works. You're not going to get a disease. You're not being punished." Like I said, logically, I know he's right, but it doesn't help. Plus he's a bit of a believer himself. When he's watching basketball and the announcer has the arrogance to claim that the player shooting free throws will undoubtedly make the shot, he springs into action. To appease the spirit who actually decides this, my husband repeats, "He's going to miss. He's going to miss." Thereby giving the power back to the spirit, who, feeling better about regaining control, lets the shot go in. My mother's friend, pretty interested and involved in the spirit world, would tell me I won't get the diseases I fear because they're not my karma. She seems to have a good relationship with the spirits so that helps a little. Then there's my yoga teacher. She doesn't quite know what my story is, but she senses some tension and tries to get me to relax. At the end of a workout, we lie down on the floor, rest our legs on a chair, and extend our arms with our palms facing up. In a receptive pose. I close my eyes and she soothingly talks to the class, getting us to relax our muscles. I'm trying hard to stop thinking, to stop worrying, and it's almost working. That is until she says, "Think about the one thing that we all share. The thing that unites us. The air we breathe." Great. TB. I flip my hands over so as not to receive. And I start to think that I might need more drugs than just vitamins and Advil. Maybe I should rethink that antipill vow of mine.

YOU TELL ME

It was probably a lot of things. Not just one monumental event. Lots of little things that finally got to him. And truthfully, I'm not sure it was the worries. Sure he'd probably prefer I wasn't quite so that way. And I think he did use the worries as his excuse to leave, but really I don't think they were it. For me they were. They were the beginning, the middle, and the end. Life would be good, perfect even, if I didn't have them. But for him I think they were like something you put up with. Some wives spent too much money, others didn't want sex enough. His had a blood thing. I'm not exactly sure what it was, what wasn't working for him. But I don't think it was the worries.

WE NEED TO TALK

I was a little nervous about how the kids were going to take the idea of my husband and me separating. I saw this Mother's Day card in a store that kind of summed up my concerns. There's this woman in a red coat with leopard fur trim. In one hand she has a cigarette and in the other her navy clutch. She's sitting in a chair talking through a glass wall to the guy she's visiting in prison. She says to him, "Have I failed so as a mother, Robert?" He looks back at her through the glass and with a somewhat exasperated look on his face says, "Richard."

We sat the kids down and tried to tell them in the most sketchy way why their father was going to be staying somewhere else. Because I think the whole truth might have made me look bad. Since, in general,

I like to tell the truth, at least to my kids, I asked my friend the heroin addict about my playing around with the facts. And she tried to explain the difference between privacy and secrecy. What you choose to keep to yourself because it's your own business versus what you're hiding. Which made sense. My kids didn't have too many questions about the split. Just sort of logistical ones like where would Dad be and when could they see him. Which we answered and then they went off to play.

EIGHT HOURS

Our daughter's birth had happened to coincide with my husband going on the job market. Which meant that he would be away from us for a couple of weeks at a time. When he would get back, feeling guilty about having left me in the lurch, he'd want to make it up to me. So he started handling the middle of the night feedings. Which worked out great for me, because I like to sleep. A lot. And over the years it just became the way it was. He took care of the middle-of-the-night needs. But now that he was gone, I suddenly had to do things I didn't really like or want to do. For instance this middle-of-the-night tending to the kids. And considering how old they are, it doesn't seem like it should be necessary. So I'll be lying in bed dreaming when all of a sudden, in a semiconscious state, I'll hear, "Daddy." Which starts out as a sweet whisper that I incorporate into my dream, but gets progressively louder until I smack the left side of the bed, which is, of course, empty. And then I'm forced to go into the other room to get the drink or tissue or whatever. And when I get back in my bed, I'm really tired, but I can't fall asleep. I just keep thinking about being separated, doing this all myself, wanting my husband back.

NO, REALLY. WHO DO YOU HAVE TO SLEEP WITH . . . ?

I decided it was time. I was tired of being alone and I thought I better get that pill. Which was easier said than done. The anxiety disorders clinic at our university hospital had a two-month wait for an initial consultation. I called every hour hoping there would be a cancellation. I figured their clients probably weren't the most dependable people. They might have every intention of making it to see the psychiatrist, but then they'd get stuck at home washing their hands over and over or turning off the stove again and again. But no, the patients kept showing up, and the nurse got tired of my calls. So she gave me the name of a local psychiatrist "known" for giving out drugs. "Call this doctor," the nurse said. "She'll be able to fit you in and give you meds." I went to see this woman a couple of times until it was clear that the nurse was mistaken about her drug-dispensing reputation. I then went back to the hospital, put my name on their list for cancellations, and within a week I was in. I spent about half an hour with the psychiatric nurse and then ten minutes with the world famous doctor who concluded our session by saying "Obsessive Compulsive Disorder subtype X, start her on one of the meds. Nice to meet you, ma'am."

HELL NO WE WON'T GO

Thirteen was a big year for me. I went to private school for the first time, I was anxiously awaiting what would be a very delayed puberty, and my parents split antagonistically. I must not have been handling it very well because the headmaster from school called a meeting with my family. I was taken out of class and brought to this room where my parents were waiting for me. They were sitting at this enormous conference room table. Next to them was the headmaster, the head of the middle school, and some guy I didn't know who turned out to be the school psychologist. They talked about how I seemed distracted and told my parents to take me to a psychiatrist or I couldn't come back to school the next year. I suppose they believed my problems were of the emotional sort and figured this would solve them. My parents obliged and found a lovely lady. If I had been inclined to share, I'm sure I would have done it with her, but I wasn't. I just sat there mute during our sessions. She would chat about her dead husband to break up the silence and after a few weeks of this,

she brought some games to our meetings so I wouldn't
have to just sit there bored. The higher-ups at school
knew I was seeing her and decided I could return the
following year. It might have been wise for the headmaster to have specified that I talk to the therapist, but
I guess the fact that I saw her was enough for him.

I've never been crazy about therapy. It's completely
counter to everything I learned about interacting with
people. Don't talk about yourself too much, ask questions about the other person, and don't badmouth your
family in public. If it weren't for the fact that everyone
is so convinced I should go, I wouldn't. I've always just
obliged to keep my friends and family off my back. I
never talk about myself much. Maybe because it seems
so contrived, or maybe it's just some subconscious
reluctance to get well. Whatever, I prefer to sit back
and listen to the therapist ramble on. But now that I
was turning over an even newer leaf, I decided to go
back to the supposed drug pusher that the nurse at the
anxiety disorders clinic referred me to. I figured she
must be good because she tortured me by not revealing
anything about herself or her opinions. I ask her,
　"Do you think I'm crazy?"
　She replies, "Do you think you are?"
　I answer, "Yes, what about you?"
　Then she says, "What do you think I think?"
　"I don't know, I'm not in your head."

She persists, "Well, what do you *think?*" We go on like this for a while and then it's time for me to leave. I think I'm doing a lot better.

ONCE UPON A TIME

So here I am, standing in front of my sink, not thrilled that sometime in the next hour or so I'm going to be taking a prescribed, mind-altering chemical. I decide to call my husband for support.

"Do you want to come over while I take my pill?" He is stunned. He really didn't think I'd take this step. So he's encouraged as well. And he wants to support me, so he drives over. When he arrives, I tell him I'm seeing the serious therapist and that I'm going to take this medicine as well. And truthfully, I'm a bit nervous about it all, and happy to have the company when I choke down my first dose. He brings me over a glass of water and I shake a capsule out of the bottle and into the palm of my hand. After I take it, he just looks at me. Looks sweetly. He walks over and puts his arms around me. He pulls me close and whispers in my ear, "I'm really proud of you." I feel his strength, return his embrace, rest my head on his shoulder and think, "1 star."

PART 4

HOW TO BE A GOOD WIFE

Don't be insane, a pain, or vain
nor mundane, arcane, or plain.
Use your brain
don't complain
no disdain
remain urbane.
Do not go against the grain.
Entertain in your domain.
Explain, sustain, and ascertain
all you find to be germane.
Clean a stain—
prepare for rain—
refrain, abstain, from the profane.
Maintain, obtain, have it pertain—
Tupperwear and cellophane.
Try hard not to be a strain
pick your guy up at the train.
Wear a chain, eat chow mein, clean with Gain,
    don't do cocaine.
Have a nice walk down the lane
run your fingers through his mane
sometimes even snake a drain
never, ever be inane.

Make your love so high octane!
that his interest will not wane.

WELCOME BACK

It's good to have him home. And a lot less difficult than I thought it would be to get him here. Not that I mean to suggest I had been overtly manipulative. Truly I hadn't. I was very subtle. But the fact of the matter is that I want him back and I want to get better. I do. I want to be happy and I want the family thing to work for us. Now it seems like we're on the right track. Everything's in place. All systems go.

BUT WHEN IT HITS THE GROUND IT ROTS

My son was playing on the kitchen floor and when I asked him to put his toys back in his bedroom, he instead put them in the empty cabinet to his right. He then informed me that this spot, this kitchen cabinet, was just for him. At first I thought he was being lazy, didn't want to carry his stuff all the way back to his toy chest. But then it occurred to me that the guy had to share a room with his sister, and a house with his parents, and even though for the most part he liked it that way, I guess occasionally even a four-year-old needs his own private space. What got me, though, was that he said I wasn't allowed to look inside. His sister could. His dad could. Just not me. And to be really sure I got it, didn't misunderstand him, he took out a piece of paper, drew a picture of me inside a circle, and put a line through it. No mommy. Then he taped it to his cabinet door. I suppose since it was the kitchen I could have called neutral territory, or just pulled rank and ripped his drawing off, but that seemed extreme. And I've got to be honest, while he was taking a bath, I did peek. It wasn't pot or girlie magazines or anything. Just a car, some school projects, and this little book he called a diary. So I let him carry on his charade. But it kind of irked me. What did I do to him?

A couple of days later, though, it came to me. My son must have blamed me for making his dad leave. And now that his dad's back and he feels safe, he can show his anger. Maybe it's inappropriate, but I'm really proud of my boy, for grasping what I believe is one of the fundamental principles in life. Thanks to my son, things are more even. Sure I had been manipulative and deceitful. But now, I'm also, more importantly, punished.

WHAT I LEARNED FROM MY HUSBAND

1. Peanut butter does not go in the refrigerator.
2. Liquid laundry detergent is just as good, if not better, than powdered.
3. If you don't rake the leaves, your lawn will die.

4. Children fall asleep faster if you give them bottles.

5. There is no shame in being almost five and needing to sleep in a diaper.

6. It is possible to eat a pint of ice cream in one sitting.

7. Frosted Lucky Charms *are* magically delicious.

LIFE WITH SEROTONIN

You can try really hard not to get better. Use all your strength and will. But when you're on the pill, you get better and there's not a whole lot you can do about it. It takes a little while to kick in, so there are about four or five weeks when you're basically taking medication for the sheer benefit of the side effects. Tired, spacey, constipated. But then it happens. Not dramatically. It comes on slowly, but you can tell. The thoughts and worries become less gripping. I guess I figured that once that began to happen I'd instantly become happy. But the startling realization I made as I was coming to my senses was that life's kind of a drag. There didn't seem to be much to it. And my rituals had been a nice diversion. Without them, I wasn't quite sure what to do with myself. This thought made my head ache. I got anxious, nervous, wondering if I was destined to live this dull and uninteresting life. But because of those damn pills, I wasn't even able to obsess about *that*.

ONE DAY AT A TIME

I called my friend the heroin addict with the good
news that my husband and I were giving the marriage
another go. She could tell I was happy about it, so she
was too. We'd both been through a lot together and her
life was getting back on track as well. She'd been clean
for a year, going to her NA meetings, working the steps.
She dumped the boyfriend, got off methadone, lost the
weight. There were complications. Like, whenever she
introduced herself to someone, she had to consciously
stop herself from following her greeting with . . . and
I'm an addict. Still, life was a lot easier for her. So I
figured she'd be a good person to seek advice from.
Because even though I'm glad to have my husband
home, glad I'm getting better, and glad things seem to
be going the way I want, I'm blue. It makes me
question things I'm not sure I should be questioning,
like, is my husband the guy for me. My friend said
something similar had happened to her when she got
clean, which initially, briefly, led her to that self-
mutilation incident and then for a while after led her
to serious self-doubt. But after the withdrawal symptoms were gone and she began regularly attending
meetings, her sadness lifted. She felt certain that the
same thing was going to happen to me. Once my body

got used to the medication and I found some new way to entertain myself. She was sure of it. I was just going to have to be patient.

BEEN THERE DONE THAT

There's early-relationship sex, married-with-kids sex, and now my husband and I were going to give reunited sex a try. Which seems to combine the nervousness of the first one with the familiarity of the second. Sort of the worst of both worlds. But I'm a sport and he was game, so we pawned the kids off on our neighbor, stripped down, and had at it. It was a pretty spirited session. We hadn't been together in a few months, not to mention there was a lot of hope and promise for the future. We thrashed around, got all sweaty, even tried a new position in honor of the occasion. When we were done, he put on his boxers, and went to do what it is he does. I stayed under the covers for a while going over the experience in my head. Believing that if I understood each movement and feeling, each touch and gasp, things would be clear. I would know whether or not he was the one for me. But then it hit me. It's sex. It's not like it's going to be a bad time. So I got dressed, went to get the kids, and figured I'd find my answer elsewhere.

More Things I Learned from My Husband

8. It's not wrong to tell someone you like his haircut even if you really don't.
9. If you turn your socks inside out, you can wear them twice.
10. The same holds true for all undergarments.
11. If you watch too much TV, you lose your imagination.
12. When a man is at work, it can be very annoying to have his wife calling all the time.

Too Much Time on My Hands

I had time to fill, a lot of it, so I started to think of ways to do that. Because really, you can just watch so much TV before it starts to get a bit dull. And because really, even though it wasn't a regular nine-to-five job, my husband did have a lot to do, and couldn't be bothered by me during the day. So after I dropped the kids off at school, I'd hang around the parking lot, like the other mothers, and hope to worm my way into their conversations and plans. They were a pretty receptive bunch, so I ended up tagging along to coffee shops and mall stores. I can't say it was a bad time, it just wasn't truly a good time. I tried other things as well, like the old standby, cleaning. I thought I'd get the house all spick-and-span and then go to the market and pick up some stuff for dinner. I'd make these elaborate meals which my husband really appreciated, but my children totally ignored. So by six-thirty when I was working on dinner number three for the kids, I decided that this course of action was way too labor-intensive for what little reward I received. I rented movies, caught up on my reading, did *The New York Times* crossword puzzle, rearranged my furniture, painted our chipping front door, wrote letters, baked cookies, stepped up my workout routine, and then ran into this old boyfriend I hadn't seen since I'd been in seclusion. He told me I looked good and I told him he did too, and he informed me that he was going to be in town for a few weeks and asked if we could get together. I had a lot of time on my hands so I said yes.

WHO YA GONNA CALL . . .

My husband and I don't have a whole lot to talk about now that I'm not so preoccupied with hygiene. Maybe this lull in our conversations isn't new. It very well might have started when we moved to Michigan, when I began lying to him about my mental state. At that point, though, the worries were still pretty engaging for me, so I didn't notice we weren't communicating. He probably knew something wasn't right, but couldn't quite put his finger on what it was. Now in our tense house, it was clear to both of us that something bad was happening. We were each, on our own, trying to figure out what was wrong. Basically, magically, wanting everything to be right between us. We'd avoid each other when we could and were way too polite when we couldn't. Hoping, I guess, that things would just sort themselves out. It was all pretty worrisome.

FLANNEL COTTON AND POLYESTER

I was cleaning out my dresser when it came to my attention that everything in the drawers was pretty darn dowdy. I didn't own one item that was made of silk, satin, or even some synthetic copy of a sexy fabric. I had piles and stacks of married woman underpants and bras. It was a little depressing that I'd stopped taking an interest in both my undergarments and my powers of seduction. So, since now I could, I went shopping. What a rush to be out in the world, alone, opening doors by myself, touching things. I did check to make sure that I didn't have any cuts on my hands, so nobody's body fluids could enter my system, and I did also check to make sure there weren't any pins in the panties, but these were small prices to pay for my freedom. So I went to this store and was approached by a woman who seemed as glad to be with me as I was to be with her. I hadn't been around too many strangers and I was excited to have the chance to hone up on my social skills. I'm not sure what her reasons were.

"Can I help you with something?" she asked me.

"You sure can. I'd like to buy something sexy." Which I learned is a rather subjective term, because she led me to this wild little red number with hooks, and snaps, and what appeared to be glitter. I don't know if I'm just out of step with fashion or if my repressed upbringing led me in a more conservative direction, but I was thinking maybe a plain black silk bra. I didn't know if I needed to expand my definition of sexy, ask her to meet me somewhere in the middle, or just get the hell out of there and stick to my Carter's. But then I had a vision of me wearing nothing but my maternity underwear and it wasn't pretty. I needed to go through with this. So I compromised. I picked out a simple but sexy bra, and let her choose the pattern. Leopard. Then I brought it home, washed it, and put it in that drawer that hours earlier had started this whole chain of events.

FUN IN THE SUN

The kids are out of school, my husband's classes are done, and now we're planning how to spend our summer vacation. Our first miniactivity is the end-of-year school picnic for the kids. All the families come, bring food, socialize. This year's is no exception except, we're there. My husband is stunned by the number of people I greet by name. "Bridget, nice to see you.

Where's Roger?" "Carrie, how'd that garage sale go?"
"Jane, we still on for coffee next week?" We sift through
the masses, find a nice spot, and set up camp. As I'm
unpacking our lunch, this funky little blond woman
comes right up to the corner of our blanket and
introduces herself. Seems she's new in town, the aunt
of a kid in my son's class, and is looking for friends. I
appreciate her boldness and I could use a good girlfriend nearby, so we exchange numbers. She lived in
New York for a time and so we figure we have things in
common. This could be fun.

Next activity. My husband wants to take a trip back
home to see his folks and show off the kids to his clan.
Which would be a great idea except for one thing. See,
when I was pregnant with my son, his parents came for
a visit, and, well, witnessed some of my odd behaviors.
Like, asking my husband if the lid on the jar of baby
food really did pop up. Was it properly vacuum sealed?
And if he hadn't heard or I couldn't be certain,
opening a series of jars until I was sure it was safe. His
mom would be holding my daughter, stroking her hair,
feeding her bits of Fruit & Fibre to pacify her. His dad
would be muttering something Spanish under his
breath. Then they'd have these long, serious discussions about how nutty I was and how my husband
should take care of the situation: force feed me medication, lock me up, look into that experimental brain

surgery option. I've moved on, but I'm not sure they have. And I don't really want to find out. So my husband takes the kids, for two whole weeks, out of town, while I stay here in town, alone.

ACT IV SCENE XIII

Night. A hotel room. Everything is dark except for the shadows made by the light of the TV. Low sounds of the news in the background. He is sitting on the bed, drinking a beer, wearing the suit he had on from his earlier business meeting. The phone rings. A woman on the other end of the line speaks.

Me: *(coyly) My husband's out of town.*
Him: *(his interest piqued) Really?*
Me: *Yup.*
Him: *Why didn't you go with him?*
Me: *I didn't want to.*
Him: *Well, what do you want?*
Me: *Sorry? (She is thrown off by his boldness, wondering if indeed he meant this as flirting.)*
Him: *(He clearly does.) Can I give you what you want?*
Me: *I'll tell you a story. When I was going through this rough time with my husband, I felt heavy. Like I was weighted down. Like there was this force pushing me so that all my movements*

took extra effort. I don't want to feel that way. I
want to be light.
Him: What can I do?
Me: I'm not sure.
Him: (he whispers) I'll think of something.

She closes her eyes and takes a deep breath. They make a plan to meet the following day. Fade to black.

A HARD MAN IS GOOD TO FIND

I am stunningly good at this. In a scary, it-shouldn't-be-my-talent, get-a-job, kind of way. I told my old boyfriend about some of the troubles in my marriage. How I'd been feeling that somehow my body wasn't my own. Like it belonged to my husband and my children. And I couldn't make decisions about it without first thinking how it would affect them and then consulting them. I know it's a pretty childish take on things and doesn't take into account the choices I made to bring me to this point, but still, it's true. I mean, I feel this way. Right now anyway. At the same time, telling *him* I feel this way, though true, is pretty manipulative. Not to mention I'm running my finger along his hand at the same time. So he comes back with, "Flirting is fine and I'll be honest, fun. I'm having a great time and I'm really attracted to you. But the one thing I will not do, no way, no how, no chance, is mess around with a married woman." And all I can think is, "Cool, a challenge." Oh yeah, and, "8 stars."

SHEER MADNESS

We're sitting around on the floor of my kitchen, because that's where I like to sit around, and talking about what we should do for dinner. My new boyfriend has had a long day, so he asks if it's okay to take his shoes and socks off. And I say it is, but it makes me nervous. Because he's letting himself get comfortable. I wonder if he's changing his mind about the sex thing. Then I'd really have to consider whether or not I'd actually mess around with him. As he removes them, he tells me that he's planning on staying in town another week, but now all I can do is focus on his unusually long toenails. I excuse myself and run to my bathroom to get my thirtieth-birthday present from my husband, my extremely sharp, extremely fancy, professional hair-cutting scissors. Which I now use for my new miniobsession, cutting friends' toenails. I bring them to my boyfriend, I beg and I plead, and I get him to agree to let me trim his. Right there in my kitchen. I take his foot, rest it on my leg, and grab his big toe.

"Be careful there, those are sharp," he says.

"Just relax, I know what I'm doing. I cut my kids' nails all the time."

"Ever draw blood?"

"Only once."

He smiles because he thinks I'm kidding and he lets me continue. But I don't pass up this opportunity to subtly find out if he's been tested. "If I do happen to draw blood . . . ?" Thankfully, he's clean.

When I'm done with the pedicure he, now apparently in the spirit of things, asks if I wouldn't mind also cutting off some of the dead skin around the toe, which I happily do, and then we order in a pizza.

FINE. YOUR DAD'S BIGGER

I'm kind of envious of my friend the heroin addict. She's a true, full-fledged, blow-out junkie. Sure, recovering, but a drug addict nonetheless. Me, I'm just neurotic. I suppose you could go as far as calling me mentally disordered or, maybe, insane, if it's a really superstraight crowd. But still, as pathology goes, mine's pretty uncool. Rock stars don't get magazine covers because they kept their audience waiting while they washed their hands twenty times. "I can't go on man, I think I left my stove on at home. I gotta go check." I don't see pretty things that aren't really there or speak to pretty people who aren't there either. I just check. And barely at all anymore. I feel pathetic. A loser amongst my fellow deviants. Like I need to do something edgy, something I can be proud of.

THE KISS

He came over on Sunday morning, with doughnuts, and *The New York Times,* and I made coffee. I placed a cup to his left and then sat down on his right. I put my head on his shoulder and rested it there for a few minutes. I felt calm, and safe, and happy. I felt that special feeling. I turned my head and looked up into his eyes. It was The Perfect Moment. Like in movies, when the feeling is so intense, you're so overwhelmed, that you forget everything, your husband, your family, that pesky moral code, and you just kiss. I moved my mouth closer to his face and I kept looking at his eyes and . . . Nothing. He would not kiss me. I couldn't believe it.

"You're really not going to do this, are you?"

"I thought I made that perfectly clear."

"But I want to, I want you." I leaned my face in and I did it. I kissed him. He didn't open his lips or kiss me back. So I kissed him again, and then one more time. I pulled my head back and looked at him. I went to kiss him one more time, on the lips, with my mouth closed, and this time he kissed me back. With tongue.

THREE POTATO FOUR

I guess now that we've done it he's not quite sure what to say, so he goes with this: "Are you doing okay?"

I reply with the standard, "Yeah."

"What are you thinking?"

"You really want to know?"

"Of course I do."

"I'm thinking that there are over forty words that rhyme with *screw* and many don't even end in *-ew.*" I pause. He's confused. I elaborate. "As opposed to, say, *fuck,* where all the rhyming words end in *-uck.*" I took out a pencil and as I recited the words out loud, I wrote them down too. For proof. "ew. ewe. boo. coo. dew. goo. who. jew. lieu. moo. new. pooh. sue. Sue. too. two. to. true. you. view. woo. zoo. flu. flew. Stu. stew. clue. eschew. renew. kazoo. zazu. crew. grew. rue. shrew. hullabaloo. drew. kerchoo. construe. blue. blew. glue. brew." I smile broadly and look his way. He still seems bewildered. Probably just due to the breakdown in *his* moral code.

JUST CHECKING TOO

Sometimes I observe my kids, purely for genetic reasons, to see if they might be coming down with some of

151

my symptoms. Like, I noticed my daughter, when she climbs stairs, first touches the right banister, then the left, then the right, then the left. Is this merely a game? Or could it be her light switch? And my son, before he goes to bed, needs to fold his clothes just so, and then put them in a pile by his feet. Which isn't too odd except that just so can be very specific. And time-consuming. I'm not sure what to do with this information. Do I hope they outgrow it or should I take them in to be tested? It's not like I want to focus too much attention on their personality quirks, but I do want to be a responsible parent. Perhaps I could be saving them some future anxiety. But that probably consists of chopping up little green and white pills and putting them in apple sauce. And I'm not crazy about that idea. So instead, I decide that when they return, I'll sit the two of them down, and tell them that there's no such thing as Santa. Then I'll ask each of them to tell me some secret they've been keeping from me. And hope that does the trick.

DIALOGUE

"You know I have to go back home tomorrow," he said.
  "I know."
  "Can I see you again? Will you call me?"
  I said, "Sure."
  "Are you going to be all right?"

"Yeah, I guess."

"What are you going to do?"

"I'm not sure."

"If you need to talk, you can call me. Any time."

"I know, thanks."

"I've really enjoyed these last few weeks."

"So have I."

"Take care of yourself."

"Okay."

"Bye then."

"Bye."

HONEY I'M HOME

My husband and kids came home from their trip, and as they walked through the door, all three of them were beaming. Glad to be home, glad to see me.

"I love you so much, Mommy. More than the whole United States," my daughter said as she ran to me and hugged me hard.

"I love you right back honey." I closed my eyes and just felt her body. Then my son ran up and joined her.

It was great to have them home. Really great. It was like the feeling I had as a kid, waking after a bad dream, and crawling into bed between my parents. I hadn't realized that there was a grown-up equivalent to this feeling. I was glad to have discovered it.

HUH?

My husband just came out with it, brought it right out in the open, laid it on the table. "What's going on here?"

I played dumb. Gave him a quizzical look.

"Seriously." He continued, "I can't live like this. We need to figure this out." But all we could figure out for the next few days was that it was easier, better, if he slept in another room. And then in another few days, figured, well, he figured it was better if he went and stayed at his friend's house. I knew that we should talk about this, about what was going on, about what I had done. Every time he called or came to get the kids I tried to tell him, but I couldn't. And since he seemed so sure that it was better to be apart and since I tended to agree with him, I just didn't open my mouth, and got carried along by his strength and resolve.

AND STILL MORE THINGS I LEARNED
FROM MY HUSBAND

13. Sticks and stones *will* break my bones.
14. An over-thirty, unemployed, divorced mother of two is not a catch.

Okay, he's mad at me. Really mad. Feel-it-from-the-pit-of-your-stomach-to-the-clench-of-your-fist mad. I understand. I told him about the boyfriend. Against the advice of almost everyone I spoke to, I should add. Their collective opinion was something like—what's the purpose? Why tell him? To appease some feeling of guilt? Because when you boil it all down, really, it's not about infidelity, it's about our relationship. But my thinking was slightly different. Sure I felt bad, but that wasn't my predominant feeling. It just seemed that my husband and I were so stuck together, so drawn to each other, so likely to coast through life with each other that without some major rift, we would wind up back together. Which didn't seem like the right move for either of us. So I told him and set things in motion.

But he did get me thinking about what I have to offer the world. I have no income, no savings, no alimony (due to my higher education and the "brief" duration of my marriage), a fifteen-hundred-dollar debt, no job prospects, no man, no car. And two kids to support. I thought it might be wise to carve out my space in the world. Make my mark. So I called up that little blond woman, made a date with her, and took out the paper to look for my own place and a source of income.

BALD IS BEAUTIFUL

There's something about the crispness of fall—and this animal push-up bra of mine—that's really brightening my day. The sky seems a little bluer, the grass a little greener, my walk a little taller. Which made it a lot easier to regain my balance when I got this call from the kindergarten teacher informing me that my kid had head lice. I went to get them both, just to be safe, and thanks to my hygienic training, knew just how to handle the situation. The teacher tried to reassure me that it's really clean heads that lice like. And when I called my mother, because that's what one does when one is overwhelmed, I could hear in her silence that she was squinting her eyes, shaking her head disapprovingly and wondering how I let my kids get such nasty varmints. Were we perhaps slumming it of late? Out of habit, I went to find their dad, for help and comfort, but he assured me that this was a one-person job. He said he'd do it or I could, but both of us was unnecessary. I growled and went home to begin the delousing. As my kids sat naked in the bathtub with chemicals on their heads, I went around the house vacuuming everything from the carpet to the phone, boiling all hair instruments, and washing all bedding and clothing that our hair might have touched. My kids kept asking, "Why do we have to stay in here?" "Why can't we wash this stuff out?" "Why are you cleaning so much?" I finally took to just saying, "Lice. Now stop asking." At the end of it all, I sighed heavily and said, "That was fun." My daughter looked up at me, smirked, and said back, "You're being sarcastic, aren't you?"

As I was lying in bed after the flurry of activity from the day it occurred to me that, apart from the nuisance of it all, I had an utter lack of caring about those little parasites in my orbit. Not that I wasn't going to follow proper procedure to try and get rid of them, but just that after that was done, I didn't feel the need to obsess about them anymore.

MI CASA

"Apartment for rent in renovated building downtown. $500 a month. Section 8 welcome."

Perfect. I called, got an appointment, and met this landlord who was nothing like the cigar-chomping, overweight type I thought he'd be. He was young, handsome, clean-cut. He looked really trustworthy. We headed up a flight of stairs, through a long hallway, and into this apartment that was small, but nice in an urban kind of way. We walked all the way in and I noticed this soft thumping of a bass, from the music played in the café downstairs, and also this faint smell of eggs, from I guess their kitchen. But it was affordable and downtown, walking distance to food and necessities, and so I overlooked the flaws, which also included chipping paint, a broken window, a funny stain on the floor, only one bedroom, and decided to take it. He said okay, we shook on it, and I had a place.

LAVERNE AND SHIRLEY

I haven't had a girlfriend in the same town as me in the longest time. What a kick. I invite her over to dinner and we make salads and grilled cheese sandwiches. She paints her nails with my daughter, draws pictures with my son, and gabs with me about boys and jobs and life in general. My daughter likes getting attention from this hip woman: it makes her feel grown up. My friend's effect on my son is a little harder to understand. He starts saying things like,

"Do you know why I'm cleaning my hands even though I'm not done with my dinner?"

"Well, no. Why?" I ask back.

"Because I'm going to rub her back." And he proceeds to put his arms up my new friend's sweater and tickle her spine. She now serves the dual purpose of being my foil and my son's object of desire. He tries to stick his tongue in her mouth and then asks her kindly if she'll lie down so he can kiss her all over her body. A far cry from the boy who, some time earlier, got

freaked out by his stiff dick. I guess it's progress.
Growing up.

I'm spending a lot of time with my new gal. Talking
on the phone, going to movies, walking around town,
looking for boys. She let me cut her bangs and I let her
use my bathroom. It was just like I imagined having a
girlfriend would be when I was sitting stuck in my
house pretending that I was happy that way. Alone and
germless. But now I see the light.

SWEET TOOTH

I was eating a piece of candy when I felt something
hard in the midst of my chewing. I got that familiar
pang in my stomach, but it's so easy to get rid of it now.
I just went through one series of mind games and then
I was past it. The candy was made by a machine, the
thing wasn't sharp, all diseases would be dead. . . .
Then I sucked the chocolate from around the object so
I could take a quick peek, just to be sure it wasn't a
needle. I held it in my hand and I swear it looked like a
tooth. Which is kind of creepy, but definitely not too
likely, so I let it go. I'm feeling pretty proud of myself,
pretty cocky, as I'm licking the remnants from inside
my mouth. But as I'm doing this, my tongue feels
something different. My stomach doesn't turn or anything, but I'm curious, so I go to the mirror to have a
look. And lo and behold, I discover it was indeed a

tooth. Mine. Now I have a gaping, jagged, half-tooth right near the front of my mouth. I'm thinking maybe I'm being revisited by my punitive God. Or maybe that guy who slammed my karma, the one who wouldn't take our LA apartment, was right. Whatever the case, I look like a hillbilly and I am not too pleased.

WHEN I GROW UP I WANT TO BE . . . A PRINCESS

I had few options on the job front. My bright idea, though, was to ask the guys in my life to supplement me. My husband agreed to pay the rent, for the kids' sake, and my dad was kind enough to cover bills until a check came in. Then I hit the help wanted page in the local paper. Nothing magical popped out at me. Nothing struck my fancy. I got sad. I put down the paper and went to the café downstairs to wallow in self-pity and drink something frothy. The guy next to me sensed my sorrow and struck up a conversation. He's new to the area, starting a business out of his home, needs clerical help, doesn't know anyone, would I be interested? I gave him a big closed-mouth grin and I had my job.

THE CALM AFTER THE STORM

Once their dad forgave me, perhaps facilitated by the young, cute girlfriend, and the raise at work, life became a lot calmer for the kids. For him. For me. Being with what he termed a "normal" girl made him happier in a much more Zen kind of way. He started saying things like, "No fight. No blame." And, "Be like water." Let go of the anger, go with the flow. That seemed to work for him. Although he occasionally lapsed into an un-waterlike state, I could hardly hold it against him. And I was glad to have the peace restored. Glad he was happy even though there was a small, ugly place deep down in my body that was grumpy and resentful. We ended up having a pretty friendly relationship. We were able to enjoy the good in each other. It was a nice, unexpected twist. His life was finally as he'd wanted it to be, how he'd envisioned it all these years. It seems getting rid of me was just what he needed. And I thought Prozac was a tough pill to swallow.

CAPITALISM RULES

This was my dad's favorite joke when I was a kid:

Second-grade teacher: Johnny, what does your dad do for a living?
Johnny: My dad's a doctor.
Teacher: And Timmy, what does your dad do?
Timmy: My dad's a fireman.
Teacher: What about your dad, Joey?

Joey: My dad's dead.
Teacher: Well, what did he do before he died?
Joey: (clutching his chest and falling to the
floor) AHHHHHHHHHHHHHHHH!

I think there's a way in which what you do defines who you are. Maybe not really, but people buy that. And while in theory there was nothing wrong with my job, it just didn't seem to go with my personality. So I started to look for another one. I tossed around the idea of drug counseling again, or making my dad happy and calling back the dean of the law school, but I was newly stable. I didn't think it was wise to test the effectiveness of my medication in such an intense way. At least not quite yet. So I took a job as a waitress. But in a special place. A bar. Not just any bar—one with a reputation for bad service and a surly waitstaff. On my second day there, I overheard this exchange:

Server: Do you need a drink?
Customer: (trying to be clever) Do I need one
or do I want one?
Server: (rolling her eyes) Would you like me to
get you a drink or would you rather just have a
semantic argument?

It is the perfect job. I get to smoke, drink, and be sarcastic all while earning an honest living.

THE MORAL OF THE STORY

My new friend told me a story. She said, "Swear to God it's true. It happened to my friend." She's laughing, because it's a funny story, but the woman, her friend it happened to, took it all really seriously. It seems this woman was on a boat trip when she ran into the sister of the first boy she ever kissed. The two spent a good part of the week together. They talked, hung out, shared stories. When the trip was about to come to an end, the sister, clearly caught up with the nostalgia of it all, asked if she could pass the woman's number on to her brother. Rekindle their childhood passion. The woman was single, a little lonely, she remembered him fondly, she said yes. Well, time passed, months in fact, and the guy did not call. My new friend's friend couldn't figure it out. But she tried. Maybe he was in love, getting over a past love, gay, really swamped at work, on a trip around the world. She called the sister under the pretense of continuing their friendship, but really, mostly, to see if she could get an answer. The sister wasn't much help. She was pretty surprised to hear that her brother hadn't called. He was single, lonely, had time on his hands. So that call makes my new friend's friend pretty sad. She starts going on about how it must be her. What's wrong with her? Why

won't he call her? She's too ugly? A really bad kisser?
What? She's getting real down about it, down on
herself. But then, one night, the guy, he calls. They
spend about a half an hour chatting and then she gets
up the nerve to ask him why it took so long to get in
touch. My new friend has to stop telling me the story
for a moment. She's pretty out of control, laughing so
hard she's having a tough time getting the words out.
But she composes herself because, well, her friend
took it all really seriously. The reason this guy didn't
phone was he had acquired a debilitating skin disorder and wanted to finish the course of medication
before calling her. So he could be more psychologi-
cally on his game. At this point, my new friend is
peeing her pants. She keeps asking me, "Am I being
mean? Is this bad?" Because her friend was stunned.
Totally taken aback by his excuse. Not that she didn't
believe him, she totally did. So did my friend and
frankly, so did I. It's just, this had not occurred to
her. She could probably have ruminated on it till she
turned blue and never thought of that one. In fact,
that's exactly what she had done.

Which brings me to the point of my story. You can
mind fuck something until it makes you crazy and it's
all wasted energy. Spending so much time in your
head. Because, the fact is, no matter what spin you
choose, you just don't know. You can't know. So go out,

have a good time, make the most of your life. And when you start to doubt yourself, if that happens, do what I do and blame it on the guy with the debilitating skin disease and let it go. Because life's just way too short to bother with such nonsense. Oh, and don't forget to take your medication. 7480 stars.